How to get   ...

to come to you

How to get clients to come to you

**A seven-stage system for
attracting and keeping clients**

Nigel Temple

WORDS AT WORK, LONDON

© Nigel Temple 2007

ISBN 978 0 9552798 1 2

Published by:

Words at Work, London
West Hill House
6 Swains Lane
London N6 6QS
United Kingdom

E-mail: info@words-at-work.org.uk
Website: www.words-at-work.org.uk

Printed and bound through:
Colorcraft Ltd, Hong Kong, China

Cover photograph:
Raymondo Marcus
(www. raymondomarcus.com)

Legal disclaimer
Nigel Temple shall not be liable for any direct, indirect, special or consequential
damages in contract, tort or otherwise, arising out of the use of this book or the
reliance on information in it. The content of this paragraph shall apply to the
maximum extent permissible by applicable laws. Any rights not expressly granted
herein are reserved. Nigel Temple has used reasonable care to ensure that the
information in this book is accurate and up-to-date. Although he has taken
precautions to prevent the occurrence of errors and omissions, the reader of this
book should not take the accuracy of the information for granted. None of the
material in this book is to be relied upon as a statement or representation of fact.
English law and jurisdiction applies with respect to contents of this book.

Dedicated to my wife, Joanna,
and our children Carly, Ben, Sophie and Will

Some comments on
How to Get Clients to Come to You

"Excellent. Bursting with ideas."

Chris Challis, Managing Director, Camwells
(www.camwells.co.uk)

"I highly recommend that you read this book. It provides a stimulating range of ideas."

Raymond Marks, Managing Director, VAR International
(www.varinternational.com)

"I have known and worked with Nigel Temple since the mid-1990s. Having met many marketing people over my 35 years in business, he is the most practical and accessible 'marketing guru' I have found. He knows his business and he knows business. I would recommend him to anyone who needs to 'kick-start' their marketing process. I recommend that you buy this book and apply what it says. Your business will benefit as a result!"

Walter Blackburn, Managing Director, PeopleTrack
(www.peopletrack.co.uk)

"Nigel Temple made a big difference to our marketing. We experienced a dramatic increase in response rates as soon as we implemented his ideas. *How to Get Clients to Come to You* is packed full of practical marketing advice. I recommend you buy this book and put the ideas to use!"

Jack Black, founder of MindStore
(www.mindstore.com)

"*How to Get Clients to Come to You* is refreshing and easy to read. It is a truly practical guide that all client-based businesses should implement to develop their business."

Glenn Watkins, Chief Executive, Ecademy
(www.ecademy.com)

"Our marketing is producing results. I am delighted to recommend Nigel Temple as a knowledgeable, results-focused marketing consultant and author."

Chris Wright, Managing Director, Skillweb
(www.skillweb.co.uk)

"If you are running a business you have to be excellent at low-cost marketing. This book shows you how to do this, step by step. Highly recommended!"

Dave Clarke, CEO, NRG Business Networks
(www.nrg-networks.com)

"Nigel Temple thinks outside the box. He gives a decisive view of the challenges facing your business and the new thinking needed to push the business forward with renewed intensity."

Tim Crabtree, Managing Director, Abbotts Office Solutions
(www.abbotts-office.com)

"I am delighted to recommend Nigel Temple and *How to Get Clients to Come to You.* His ideas have proved to be of great help to our company."

Graham Hill, Joint Managing Director, Verbatim
(www.thephoneansweringservice.co.uk)

CONTENTS

FOREWORD

The sole purpose of business is to create and keep customers and clients. This basic truth is often forgotten as businesses focus on short-term transactional sales, rather than on building long-term relationships with their clients.

Nigel Temple's seven-stage approach to attracting and retaining clients takes you back to basic principles – understanding who your target customers are, what your point of differentiation is and how you communicate that clearly, consistently and concisely. It is about securing preference and building sustainable relationships, by doing what you say you will do, day in and day out.

Your ability to think, analyse situations, make decisions and implement them is the key determining factor of your profitability. To help you hone these skills, this book highlights some simple yet effective principles for business success.

How to Get Clients to Come to You is a thoroughly practical assessment of trusted techniques that you can use to create and keep clients. It is a welcome balance of insight and practicality that also embraces modern communications tools and techniques.

Paul Gostick
Chairman
The Chartered Institute of Marketing (CIM)

The objective of this book is to help you
to **attract more clients** by
generating **more conversations**
with people who want to know
how you can help them.

INTRODUCTION

How to Get Clients to Come to You describes a system for
attracting and keeping clients. With the emphasis on
practical and proven techniques, the book is the
culmination of my working with client-based businesses
for more than 25 years. If you own or work for a
client-based business, then this book is for you.

Specifically, the book is aimed at:

- Business owners and directors
- Marketing professionals
- Service professionals
- Added-value product providers
- Anyone interested in sales lead generation

What is the difference between a 'client' and a 'customer'?
A 'customer' is someone who buys from you once, so there
isn't much chance of developing a relationship. A 'client',
however, buys from you regularly. The number of client-
based businesses is growing enormously. Sadly, this means
that you are probably facing increasing competition. The
good news, though, is that you are reading this book!

How to Get Clients to Come to You presents a seven-stage system.

STAGE 1: Visualise a client-rich future
When I meet people seeking advice on marketing, I ask
if they have a clear vision of where they're going and a
burning desire to get there. I watch carefully as they reply.

This 'vision of a successful future', combined with the determination and drive to get there, will propel you forward through the calm waters and storms that lie ahead. Stage 1 involves using your right brain and shows you how to develop a clear vision of the future of your enterprise.

STAGE 2: Think in detail

You are caught up in an endless stream of meetings, e-mails, computer time, telephone conversations and travel. It's all too easy to become hypnotised by activity. When do you get time to stop and think? Stage 2 involves using your left brain and is about taking time out to write your marketing plan. You can write a plan in a morning.

STAGE 3: Apply client-attraction laws

You now have a clear vision of where you are going and how to get there. It's time to apply the principles that underlie successful marketing. These include creativity, building relationships, repetition, integration, follow-up and responsiveness – all powerful means of attracting and keeping clients. Successful marketing also rests on your ability to turn your clients into advocates, to become a useful information source and to promote reciprocity.

STAGE 4: Use internet marketing

Your clients will expect you to have a website. This is where current clients will look for new ideas and information, and where prospective clients will check you out before they give you a call. So your website is a key element of your marketing strategy. Stage 4 looks at practical ways to make your website work harder for you. We also discuss opt-in e-mail marketing, a highly effective client-attraction technique.

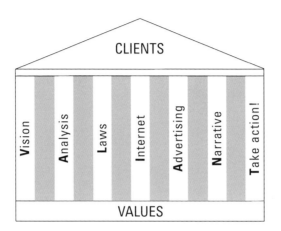

FIGURE 1: The seven stages involved in attracting clients, underpinned by a set of values (e.g., commitment, honesty, integrity and professionalism)

STAGE 5: Use low-cost promotional techniques
There are many traditional ways to promote your business, including networking, mailing, referrals, PR and organising events. In Stage 5 the emphasis is on low-cost marketing methods, often the most effective way of attracting clients. This section is packed full of practical tips and ideas.

STAGE 6: Write compelling words
The words used in marketing materials such as advertisements, websites, leaflets and mailshots are called 'copy'. Most marketing communication revolves around the written word, so it's important to write compelling copy. Stage 6 describes practical and painless ways to improve your copy.

> It's never too late to be what you might have been.
> *George Eliot (novelist)*

STAGE 7: Take action!

Businesses tend to fall into two groups. The people in the first group know that:

> *If they always do what they've always done,*
> *They will always get what they've always got.*

They ask questions, but don't over analyse. They've tried other approaches, but these haven't produced results. They're ready for a change. They come up with plans, ideas and techniques and they implement them. The people in the second group procrastinate. They spend a lot of time talking about what they are going to do. They worry about perfection. And little or nothing happens. Their marketing plan never gets off the runway.

An understanding of the techniques is not enough. The successful marketer must get up and do something. *How to Get Clients to Come to You* will work only if you put the ideas into action.

I hope that you enjoy reading this book. I suggest that you:

- keep it on your desk
- highlight the things you need to do
- take action!

Good luck with your marketing.

Business owners / senior management must be
committed to marketing.
If that commitment isn't there,
marketing won't work.

Marketing is a **journey**, not a destination.
It revolves around a deep **understanding of clients**.
The purpose of marketing is to **create and keep clients**.
Always **focus on the client**.
Organise around clients and their needs.

Stage 1

VISUALISE A CLIENT-RICH FUTURE

Before you create sustained external success, you must create internal success. Winning sportsmen and women know this. So do salespeople, actors and professionals from all fields of endeavour. This section on visualising a client-rich future is crucial to your marketing.

Think of marketing as the visible surface of your enterprise. If you step back and think about it, for many client-based businesses it's only the marketing side that people see – the branding, website, e-mails, leaflets and mailshots. When you talk to prospective clients on the phone, they're hearing you in 'marketing mode'; when you meet them in person your body language goes into 'marketing mode'.

In order to succeed out there in the world of marketing, you need to tune into your Inner Marketer. This is the part of you that will drive your marketing communications and campaigns forward. For this part to work effectively, you need to have a strong belief in yourself and your products / services, you need to be able to visualise where you are going and you need be aware of the qualities that attract clients.

Self-belief

Do you have a strong belief in yourself and your abilities? Success is first and foremost a mental attitude. Clients are attracted to people who feel successful. And this feeling comes from inside you. This is your Inner Marketer.

If you want more clients, start by thinking about a client-rich future, a successful future. You can do this through visualisation or by writing. I suggest that you try both approaches, because you'll then be using both hemispheres of your brain – the right brain, which thinks in pictures, and the left brain, which processes words, numbers and detail.

The right side can visualise the future. It thinks in pictures, which is why we see images in our dreams. Much of our behaviour and actions are generated unconsciously. By tapping into the power of the right side of your brain, you can create a compelling vision of a client-rich future. This will change your behaviour and drive you forward in everything you do. You'll find yourself spending more time on client-generating activities. Your fears will diminish. New business relationships will materialise. You will attract more clients.

Right and left brain exercises

Right brain visualisation works best when you're relaxed. Close your eyes and focus on your breathing. Think about the breath coming slowly into and out of your body. Hold your breath for a moment when you exhale and when you inhale. After a minute or two your brain will calm down and you'll find that it is easier to visualise your future.

Now imagine being inundated with people who want to work with you. You are so busy that you have to turn people away. Imagine, in detail, the clients that you'll have. See yourself delivering an excellent and sought-after service. Think about the benefits for your clients. Imagine the income you'll earn and how you'll spend it.

Take a few moments and do this 'imagining' exercise now. Then do it a couple of times a day for the next three weeks. You might find it easier to do the exercise early in the morning, or it might work better for you later on in the day.

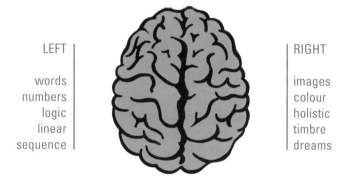

LEFT

words
numbers
logic
linear
sequence

RIGHT

images
colour
holistic
timbre
dreams

FIGURE 2: The human brain, with its logical left side and visual right side

The left brain processes words, numbers and logical thinking. Using this approach, write down what a client-rich future will be like. Describe the types of clients you'll have and the sort of work you'll do with them. List the benefits they'll get from working with you. Write down how much money you'll make and what you'll spend it on. (In Stage 2 we look at the marketing plan, where the left brain comes into its own.)

Some people can simply close their eyes and visualise. Others find it helpful to write. Interestingly, when they write, the pictures often start to come. But don't be

---

I am enough of an artist to draw freely upon my imagination. Imagination is more important than knowledge. Knowledge is limited. Imagination encircles the world.
Albert Einstein (scientist)

concerned if they don't – your unconscious mind will start doing the work for you.

Don't fall into the trap of thinking, "Oh yes, I get it", and then not do the exercises. Understanding what you've just read is one thing. Doing the exercises is an entirely different experience. They take only a few minutes and they won't cost you any money. This is one of the most productive things that you will ever do for yourself and your business.

Think about it: if you aren't convinced that you are a client magnet, who else will be? Prospective clients? Movers and shakers? The people you network with? Client attraction is largely an 'inside job'.

Attraction

Pause for a moment and think about the people to whom you're attracted:

- What characteristics do they have?
- How long did it take you to 'sum them up' when you first met them?
- What made you decide that you'd get along with them?
- Were your first impressions accurate?

I have asked thousands of seminar delegates these questions. Most of them say that, on meeting someone for the first time, it takes between 1 and 10 seconds to give them a mental 'thumbs up' or 'thumbs down'. Frightening, isn't it?

Why are we attracted to certain people? Is it the clothes they wear? The way they move? Perhaps it's the way they talk? These are all contributing factors. The answer, however, doesn't lie on the surface. The real reason that we're attracted to certain people comes from within them. So before we get to work on the visible side of your business (branding, websites, leaflets, etc.), we must ensure that you're tuned in – on the inside!

Some of the qualities that attract clients are listed in Box 1. If you apply these qualities to your thinking, organisation

BOX 1

Qualities that attract clients

Accountability	Helpfulness	Punctuality
Adaptability	Honesty	Resourcefulness
Brand	Humour	Respect
Capability	Innovation	Service
Charisma	Integrity	Simplicity
Commitment	Intelligence	Speed
Communication	Knowledge	Straightforwardness
Creativity	Learning	Success
Decisiveness	Openness	Systems
Excellence	Optimism	Teamwork
Expertise	Passion	Technology
Focus	Performance	Tenacity
Friendliness	Politeness	Trust
Fun	Positive	Truth
Hard work	Professionalism	Value

That's quite a list, isn't it? How many of these qualities apply to you and your business?

and products / services, you'll find that clients are naturally attracted to you and will be happy to refer you to others. You will have created a beneficial cycle which will keep you 'client rich' for years to come.

Fear of failure

Here are some of the things that client-orientated businesses say about marketing:

- "It's expensive, isn't it?"
- "We don't know what will work and what won't."
- "We tried running some adverts / mailshots / events once but they didn't work."

So they either stop marketing or they don't invest enough time and energy in it. Does this sound like you?

Do not fear mistakes. There are none.
Miles Davis (jazz musician)

Since 1986, I've worked with more than 10,000 seminar delegates and more than 1000 clients. I am always interested to know what they do with the ideas that I teach.

Some of them forge ahead and rapidly implement the ideas. For example, they start using 'client-attraction techniques', they make changes to their website and they start experimenting with new promotional concepts.

A significant group of people, however, never really get started. They tell me that they are "thinking about it" and

> Use the secrets of **client attraction**
> **Imagine the clients** and the cash
> Get up, move and **take massive action**
> And you'll soon whizz past others in a dash!

making plans. Quite often, they never actually do anything. Or, if they do, the plans are half-hearted versions of what they learnt. Why is this? Perhaps it's because although marketing is important, it is seldom urgent. Clients, staff and raising invoices are urgent. Marketing can wait until tomorrow… Can't it?

Thinking, talking and planning are important. But if you want to attract clients you must take action – and keep on taking it. And the time to start is right now.

CHAPTER SUMMARY

Tune into your Inner Marketer – Create a vision of a client-rich future – Do visualisation exercises regularly – Reflect on what attracts one person to another – Beware of the fear of failure – Don't procrastinate – Take action now

Stage 2

THINK IN DETAIL

A marketing plan doesn't take long to produce. It will mean, however, that you will have to take time out of the 'business battle' in order to sit down and think. And it will be well worth the effort!

Stage 1 focused on creating a picture of a client-rich future. This image was generated by the right side of your brain. Now it's the turn of your logical left brain, which processes the details.

The left brain works with chunks of information, such as words and numbers. It thinks sequentially, one step at a time. It is the home of logical thinking. Therefore, it's the left brain that will fill in the details of your marketing plan.

The time challenge

Do you have time to think and plan? If you want to become successful and stay there, you must do this. It is time well spent. So reach for your diary and schedule some planning time, along these lines:

Annually: Spend one or two days on marketing planning
Quarterly: Spend half a day reviewing your marketing plan
Monthly: Devote an hour or two to marketing thinking and planning
Daily: Do some marketing

A concise plan

You already have your business plan, don't you? (If not, this is a good time to do one.)

Your marketing plan should stand alone as a complete document. It should also fit into the big picture – your business plan.

A marketing plan should be concise, just a few pages long (although the thinking can be as big as you like). Big plans take too long to produce. They can create a trap – paralysis by analysis. You have to update them, which is time consuming. And anyway, who has the time to read them?

I recommend that you create a micro marketing plan that:

- you keep by your side
- you review once a month
- will help you to achieve your goals

BOX 2

Mind Mapping®

Mind Maps® are very useful at the planning stage. They are a graphical way of sorting out your thoughts.

As you capture your key ideas on a sheet of paper, a Mind Map® will help you to see the big picture (*see* Figure 3, overleaf).

Take a look at the world bestseller, *Use Your Head,* by Tony Buzan (*see* Appendix 3) or go to www.nigeltemple.com for an article on the subject.

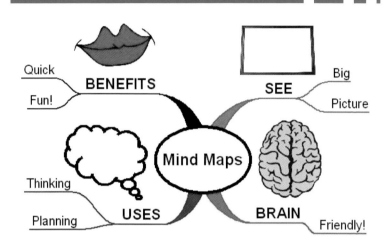

FIGURE 3: The benefits of Mind Mapping

Key elements

The key elements of your marketing plan should include:

- objectives
- competitive analysis
- segmentation
- differentiation
- products and services
- pricing
- geographical coverage
- promotional mix
- marketing budget
- measurement

Objectives

Spell out what you want your marketing to deliver, particularly:

- projected turnover
- profit goals

One of your key objectives should be to build a trusted brand name for your business. When we make purchasing decisions, we tend to go for names we recognise, names we know will deliver their promises.

A brand = a promise

Once you've established a recognisable brand name:

- clients will come to you
- they will be happy to pay higher prices
- your business will be worth more (should you wish to sell it)

Competitive analysis

If you don't understand the competitive 'market space' in which you operate, how will you be able to:

- stand out from the crowd?
- create key messages?
- produce unique 'value propositions'?

You probably know who many of your competitors are. If you study your main competitors closely (*see* Appendix 1), however, you'll have a much better understanding of how to position yourself in the marketplace.

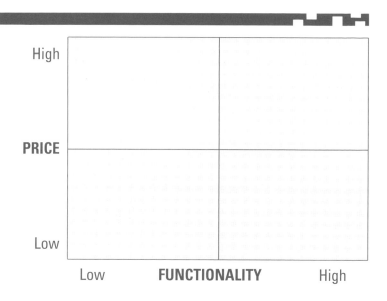

FIGURE 4: A positioning grid

An easy way of doing this is to draw a 'positioning grid' (*see* Figure 4).

Now choose one of your products / services. On the grid, mark a point on the vertical axis that represents your price position, compared with your competitors. If, for example, you are a little more expensive than your competitors, mark a point just above the halfway line.

Now mark another point along the horizontal axis. This represents the main features of your product / service, compared with your competitors. These features are likely to include response times, guarantees and specialist knowledge – that is, anything that contributes to the total proposition that you are offering to the marketplace.

Next, put an X where the two points meet on the grid. If your products / services are high priced and offer lots of features, the X will be in the top right hand corner of the grid. Now ask yourself two questions:

- Are you where you want to be on the positioning grid?
- How many competitors have their Xs close to you?

If you occupy a crowded market position, it will be difficult making your marketing messages heard. It's better to occupy 'clear blue water' and not be jostled by too many competitors.

BOX 3

Some tips on positioning

Swim up-market. When it comes to positioning, it's usually better to 'swim up-market' – that is, improve the quality of your product / service and increase your price. By the way, 'up-market' is where you'll have most fun (and make most money).

Choose a benchmark competitor. A 'benchmark competitor' is someone who is already where you want to be. You can emulate their marketing strategy and tactics (*see* Appendix 1).

Analyse your clients. Carry out some market research. Talk to the type of people you'll be marketing to and find out what their needs are. A revealing question to ask them is: "What annoys you most about this type of product / service?"

Segmentation

Smart businesses focus on niche market segments. Think hard about this – it may be the single most important thing you do. It won't be profitable to try to sell your products / services to everyone. Focus on the market segments that you can serve better than your competition.

A market segment = a group of people with shared needs

Start by analysing your client list and looking for patterns. If you market to other businesses, you can target 'vertical'

Identifying your market segment

I was talking to one of my clients about her sales and marketing database. "How many records should I buy?" she asked.

"Well," I replied, "the first question is: Which segments do you want to focus on? Once we've figured that out, it will help with key messages, what to put on your website homepage, where you should network and how you should populate your database. And that's just for starters!"

We then spent an hour or so talking about her previous clients and how they formed distinct clusters. We discussed the types of clients she liked working with. We considered which industries had the most cash and which looked likely to prosper over the following few years.

"That was most interesting," she said when we had drawn some conclusions. "I'm beginning to see how powerful segmentation could be for my business."

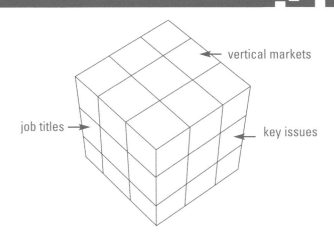

FIGURE 5: A segmentation box, illustrating market segments

markets (e.g., the automotive or pharmaceutical industries) and / or job titles (e.g., Managing Director or Finance Director). (*See* Figure 5.)

This is not to say that you should turn business away. If you have limited time, money and resources, however, it will be more productive to focus your marketing on defined segments. In this way the people you're targeting will be more likely to receive your marketing messages. When they need your type of product / service, they will be more likely to contact you.

Research is the starting point for marketing.
Without research, a company enters a market like a blind man.
Philip Kotler (marketing guru and author)

Differentiation

In a competitive marketplace, can you stand out from the crowd? The answer is, "Yes, of course you can." Here are some steps to take to differentiate your business from others:

• try to find out as much as you can about the products / services that competing businesses are offering, what their key messages are and how they position themselves

• think about what you could offer that they don't (e.g., additional services; bundled products; additional support; added value; flexible financial terms; faster delivery; more convenience; and better guarantees)

• brainstorm this issue with your colleagues

• ask your clients what they want from you

• raise your personal profile (bearing in mind that you are a unique individual, this strategy will help to differentiate your business from the rest)

• use consistent branding

• educate prospective clients about your products / services and your solutions

Once you have created points of differentiation, you should:

• create an effective 'elevator pitch' (i.e., a statement which tells people what your business is and what it delivers)

- decide on your key marketing messages, which you'll subsequently use in all your promotional techniques

- write effective headlines and straplines

The benefits of carrying out these activities will include:

- enhanced word-of-mouth marketing
- clearer positioning in your marketplace
- more enquiries
- more business

 BOX 5

Elevator pitch

Your competitive analysis and decisions on segmentation and positioning should help you to decide on your elevator pitch – what your business is and what it delivers.

As an exercise, write an elevator pitch (100–150 words) for your business.

The phrase 'elevator pitch' is based on the idea that you are one of two people in an elevator (lift) and you have the time span of the ride between floors (about 30 seconds) to deliver your pitch.

Products / services

List all your products / services. Which ones are rising and which ones are falling away? Which of them do you want to focus on? Which one do want to become well known for?

Pricing

Pricing is a key issue. It's worth getting external advice on this. Are you operating on a 'cost-plus' basis (i.e., adding up your costs and adding a gross profit percentage on top) or on 'market-based' pricing (i.e., researching the market to determine the price at which products / services like yours sell)? The latter is better.

You can increase your price if you add more value to your product / service by, for example:

- improving your product / service (and then continuing to improve it)
- offering a strong, up-front guarantee
- making your product / service available from various locations
- delivering your product / service when and where it suits clients

BOX 6

Creating a Trojan horse

Decide what product or service you can offer for free or at a low cost. This will become your 'Trojan horse'.

An example of a Trojan horse would be a free consultancy session (there's more on this in Stage 3).

Once you have established a relationship with clients via your Trojan horse, it will be much easier to attract new clients.

In general, it's better to add value and go for a higher price. Your product / service will then be perceived as being of higher quality.

Geographical coverage

How far afield do you want to travel to see your clients? It's generally a good idea to focus on business opportunities that are closer at hand. This approach can save you a considerable amount of travelling time (and is, of course, much 'greener').

Promotional mix

Decide which promotional techniques you'll use to create awareness and generate sales enquiries (most of the rest of this book is devoted to this subject). Take care to integrate these techniques so that your promotional mix has a coherent look and feel and gives you cross-selling opportunities.

Marketing budget

Draw up a detailed marketing budget for the next 12 months, showing budgeted costs for each promotional technique. For each month there should be three columns:

| Budget | Actual | Difference |

At the end of the month insert what you actually spent alongside the budget figure. This gives you the difference (*see* Figure 6).

Marketing budget

		May			June			
		Budget	Actual	Diff	Budget	Actual	Diff	TOTALS
Database	List acquisition	0			0			0
	Data validation	0			0			0
Direct mail	Direct mail letters	0			0			0
	Direct mail postcards	0			0			0
Internet marketing	Website redesign	0			0			0
	Email marketing	0			0			0
	SearchEngineMarketing	0			0			0
Networking	Membership fees	0			0			0
	Attendance fees	0			0			0
Seminars	Room hire	0			0			0
	Refreshments							
	Handouts	0			0			0
Press Relations	Copywriting	0			0			0
	Meeting journalists	0			0			0
MONTHLY TOTALS		0	0	0	0	0	0	0

FIGURE 6: An example of a marketing budget

28

Measurement

Build a monitoring procedure into your marketing plan so that you can see which promotional techniques are working and which ones are not. For example, when you receive a new sales enquiry, always ask how they found you and note down this information.

Results and feedback need to be gathered on a monthly basis so that you can take appropriate action – amend your marketing plan and implement the new approach accordingly.

CHAPTER SUMMARY

Set aside time to produce a concise marketing plan – Use Mind Mapping – Start with your objectives – Think about the brand – Analyse the competition – Choose your market position – Decide on your market segments – Differentiate your business from others – List your products / services – Set your price – Decide on the geographical area to cover – Choose a coherent mix of promotional techniques – Draw up a marketing budget – Build monitoring into the plan

Stage 3

APPLY CLIENT-ATTRACTION LAWS

You now have a vision of your client-rich future. You have also created a concise and coherent marketing plan. The next stage is to apply proven client-attraction laws. If you do this, your marketing will be far more efficient and effective.

Becoming the guru of your marketplace

A great way of attracting clients is to provide helpful, useful information. Buyers need information before they can make a decision. In a crowded marketplace, businesses that provide accessible, client-focused information will attract a greater share of enquiries.

Ask yourself this question: What would my current and prospective clients like to learn more about?

Jot down whatever immediately springs to mind. Follow this up with a brainstorming session with your colleagues / advisers on what information and advice you could provide.

Then think about ways to get this information to your clients. These could include postcards, leaflets, booklets and books – all powerful, low-cost, client-generation tools. They could also include electronic tools such as e-booklets (*see* page 36), websites and e-newsletters (*see* Chapters 4.1 and 4.2).

All these tools should provide your contact details, but they should not contain sales messages. Your job is to educate first, then sell.

Postcards

Postcards are an effective form of marketing communication, for several reasons:

- unlike letters, there is no 'opening decision'; the postcard is right there, in front of the recipient, begging to be read

- think of the postcard as an advertisement; one side carries a headline and / or an interesting image, and the other carries your advertising text

- postcards are more attention grabbing than a dull-looking letter, their images and colour appealing to the right side of the brain

- they conjure up pleasant associations (with holidays and exotic places)

- they aren't expensive

Think of postcards as information products:

- make your postcards interesting, informative and useful; they'll be much more likely to be read

- useful postcards will be kept (in the same way that a handy promotional gift will be kept), so think hard about how you can make your postcards useful

- don't forget to put your contact details on each postcard, including telephone numbers, e-mail address and website address

- you can test your postcard design very cheaply by printing them yourself

- once you have some ideas for postcards, circulate them around the office and / or to some of your contacts and clients, for their feedback

- when you've received and incorporated the feedback, think about how many postcards you need and how they should be printed (traditional offset lithographic printing or, for smaller runs, digital printing)

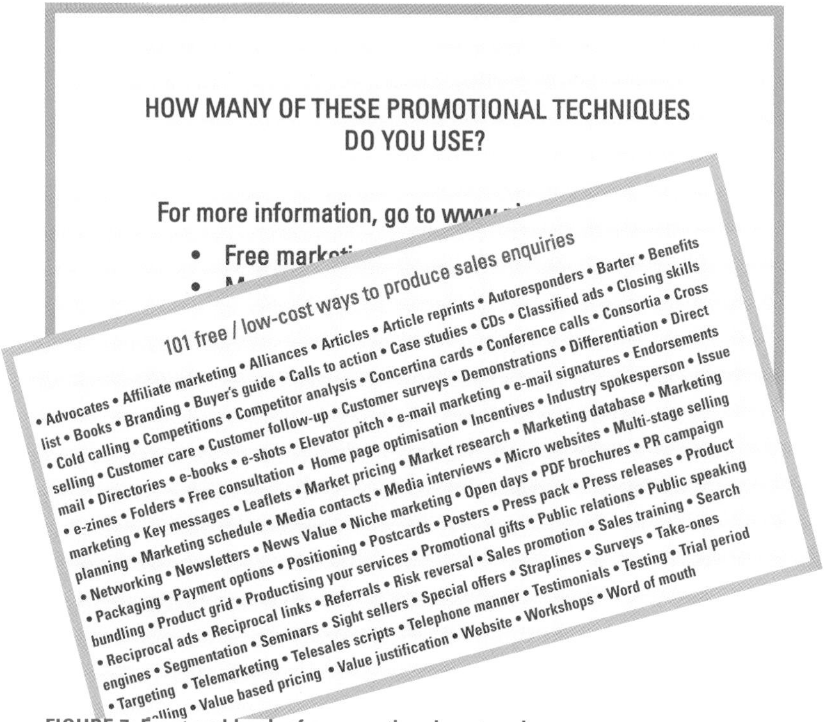

HOW MANY OF THESE PROMOTIONAL TECHNIQUES DO YOU USE?

For more information, go to www.~~~~~~

- Free mark~~~~~~
- M~~~~~~

101 free / low-cost ways to produce sales enquiries

• Advocates • Affiliate marketing • Alliances • Articles • Article reprints • Autoresponders • Barter • Benefits list • Books • Branding • Buyer's guide • Calls to action • Case studies • CDs • Classified ads • Closing skills • Cold calling • Competitions • Competitor analysis • Concertina cards • Conference calls • Consortia • Cross selling • Customer care • Customer follow-up • Customer surveys • Demonstrations • Differentiation • Direct mail • Directories • e-books • e-shots • Elevator pitch • e-mail marketing • e-mail signatures • Endorsements • e-zines • Folders • Free consultation • Home page optimisation • Incentives • Industry spokesperson • Issue marketing • Key messages • Leaflets • Market pricing • Market research • Marketing database • Marketing planning • Marketing schedule • Media contacts • Media interviews • Micro websites • Multi-stage selling • Networking • Newsletters • News Value • Niche marketing • Open days • PDF brochures • PR campaign • Packaging • Payment options • Positioning • Postcards • Posters • Press pack • Press releases • Product bundling • Product grid • Productising your services • Promotional gifts • Public relations • Public speaking • Reciprocal ads • Reciprocal links • Referrals • Risk reversal • Sales promotion • Sales training • Search engines • Segmentation • Seminars • Sight sellers • Special offers • Straplines • Surveys • Take-ones • Targeting • Telemarketing • Telesales scripts • Telephone manner • Testimonials • Testing • Trial period ~~~~~~lling • Value based pricing • Value justification • Website • Workshops • Word of mouth

FIGURE 7: Front and back of a promotional postcard

- initially, you could send just one postcard to each of your target group. But it's worth considering producing a sequence of postcards. The ideal number is seven (to find out why, *see* Chapter 3.4).

- as well as posting the postcards, you could hand them out at networking events and at meetings with current and prospective clients

- you could also ask reciprocal marketing partners to post them to their clients or to include your postcards in their mailings (naturally, you will reciprocate) (*see* Chapter 3.2)

- when you give the postcards to contacts and clients, ask if they'd like some extra ones to give to their contacts

Leaflets

Leaflets are an alternative to postcards. Even if it's a small leaflet, there will be more room available for your words than on a postcard, because you don't have to leave space for the address and a stamp.

BOX 7

Producing a Top Tips leaflet

An effective idea is to produce a leaflet containing some Top Tips about your product / service. Here's the recipe:

1. Hold a brainstorming session to produce 10–20 Top Tips about your product / service
2. Make them useful, informative and helpful
3. Add your contact details and some information about your business
4. Design and print a few copies, and test them out
5. Incorporate the feedback and print the quantity you need
6. Publicise your FREE TOP TIPS leaflet
7. Promote the Top Tips on your website in exchange for contact details (*see* Chapter 4.1)

This idea will help you to build up your database of contacts.

Booklets

With publishing software for computers now commonplace, have a go at producing your own booklet. It doesn't have to be a masterpiece of writing. It just needs to contain useful information written in a straightforward way. If writing isn't your strength, enlist the help of a professional copywriter.

Once you've written the content, choose your booklet size. Don't forget to add page numbers. For more on using publishing software to produce materials such as booklets, refer to *What Not To Write* by Kay Sayce (*see* Appendix 3).

An important part of your booklet will be the front cover. You could use clipart to produce an attention-grabbing front cover. Or there are graphic designers who specialise in book design – why not ask one for a quote?

e-booklets

The most common form of e-booklet is the Adobe® PDF file format of a printed book (visit www.adobe.com).

If you use the PDF format:

- your layout, text and illustrations will appear exactly as you want them to

- the reader can't 'copy and paste' your content (as long as you have locked the file)

- the document can be saved only in the PDF format

- you can include bookmarks for easy navigation in the documents

Books

Someone once said to me that a business book is the ultimate business card! This is true. But do you like writing? Does your business suit being linked to a book? And would a book be good for your business? If the answer to all three questions is "Yes", then this is a project worth thinking about.

Begin by analysing the books in your area of expertise that are currently in print; have a good look round the business book section in a major bookshop. Your mission is to come up with something that is as different as possible.

Find out which publishers produce books for this market segment; a good source of information for this if you live in the UK is the *Writers' and Artists' Yearbook* (*see* Appendix 3). You could also ask your network of contacts if they know any publishers who might be suitable or anyone who works in a publishing house who could offer advice.

CHAPTER SUMMARY

Provide helpful, useful information to attract enquiries – Decide which information tools to use – Make your postcards useful and attractive – Try producing a Top Tips leaflet – Have a go at compiling a booklet – Think about the advantages of e-books – Write a business book, the ultimate business card!

3.2 Promoting reciprocity

'Give to get'. This is reciprocity. It is as much a philosophy of life as it is a hard-headed marketing tactic. It seems that in this life the more you give the more you will receive. Many famous companies have built their business on the 'free sample', and thousands of businesses use this approach with great success. By offering something for free (e.g., a sample product, a special offer, free information), you are:

• making it easy for people to try out your product / service
• tapping into the power of reciprocity

'Try before you buy' is a proven marketing technique. After all, how can prospective clients make a buying decision until they've seen your product or experienced your service?

BOX 8

The power of reciprocity

The power of reciprocity is well understood in the Middle East and in Japan. If you do business in these parts of the world, you will probably encounter the Business Gift. These businesses know that a gift starts a chain of giving and receiving – which is simply good business practice.

Reciprocity is all about giving and receiving. If you give without thought of return, you tap into the 'hearts' and not just the 'minds'. Apart from the commercial justification for this, isn't it just a good way to live?

Some people think that offering free products / services will lose them business. My experience, however, is that prospective clients react well to this approach, and you end up gaining far more than you give away. But if you want to spend your life cold calling…

Offers

Offers can be used to start new relationships and to cement the relationships you have with existing clients.

Think about supermarkets. What sort of offers do they have? Here are a few examples:

- 3 for 2
- Buy one get one free (known in the trade as a 'BOGOF')
- Buy one and get (*something else*) free
- 10% off
- Extra points
- Try a sample for free

Supermarkets measure everything. They wouldn't use offers if this approach didn't work. They try hard to get you to:

- try something for the first time
- buy a larger version
- revisit a brand you haven't tried for some time

Offers are a great way of tempting people to try out your product / service. When I talk about offers in my seminars, often the first thing that people think about is some type of discounting. You should avoid discounting, however, as it tells your market that you are willing to drop your price. This leads to all sorts of unfortunate consequences.

Two examples of sales-generating offers are: free consultation and free information products.

Free consultation

Do you have to put yourself in front of people in order to make a sale? If the answer is "Yes", then instead of positioning yourself as a salesperson, why not position yourself as a consultant? For example, you could offer a one-hour free consultation.

But here is a word of warning. If you do offer a consultation session, it must be a proper consultancy session, not a sales pitch. It's fine to deliver a brief 'pitch' at the end of the session (but *do* make it brief).

Tell prospective clients in detail what they can expect from this session. One way to do this is to create a web page.

Free information products

Providing useful information via such products as postcards, leaflets, websites and e-newsletters will bring rewards (*see* Chapters 3.1, 4.1 and 4.2).

Reciprocal marketing partnerships

Why climb the mountain on your own, when you can get others to pull you to the top? Most businesses struggle along on their own, doing all their own selling and promotion and spending all their own money doing it.

Form as many reciprocal marketing partnerships (RMPs) as you can. You'll then be able to tap into your partners' existing business relationships – relationships that have cost them a great deal of money to build over many years and are based on service, integrity and trust.

Set up RMPs with like-minded business people who:

- serve the same type of clients as you do
- don't compete directly with you
- operate in the same geographical area (if you need to meet clients)

 BOX 9

My RMPs

Being in the marketing industry, I look for partners among businesses that are also in this industry. I have RMPs with business owners in:

Advertising	PR consultancy
Direct mail	Publishing
Graphic design	Telemarketing
Market research	Web development

I also have RMPs among businesses outside my industry:

Accountancy	Recruitment
Cost-reduction consultancy	Training
IT support	Translation

One of the reasons that this idea works so well is that most people prefer to do business with businesses that have been *recommended* to them. If you were thinking about going out for a meal and a friend told you about a great new restaurant, isn't it likely that you would consider going there?

Choose your partners

I have experimented with approaching companies that don't know me with the offer of a marketing partnership, but this has proved to be a struggle.

It's far more rewarding to look for partners among people you know. Start by thinking about your current business contacts and whom you could approach. If you don't have enough contacts, then this is a good reason to get out there and start networking! (For more on networking, *see* Chapter 5.1.)

I recommend RMPs to all my clients. I've found that if you launch four RMP initiatives, on average one of them will 'deliver the goods.' The others either won't really get started or will soon fade away. But the one that works will make this initiative well worthwhile.

Get RMPs airborne

Once RMPs are up and running, here are some things that you can do for your partners (and that they, in turn, can do for you):

- recommend them to your current and prospective clients
- hand out their business cards

- set up hyperlinks to each other's websites
- include their leaflets in your direct mail campaigns

If the relationship is going well, you could also consider running joint events, such as seminars.

CHAPTER SUMMARY

Apply the 'give to get' philosophy – Let clients 'try before they buy' – Tempt people with offers, such as a free consultation or free information – Build reciprocal marketing partnerships – Choose your partners carefully – Think what you can do for your partners, and vice versa – Run joint events

Your clients are travelling along a road. They start their journey without knowing you. At some stage, they hear your name. If you're lucky, they'll knock on your door and ask for some information. You'll sell something to some of these people and they will become customers. You will, if you apply proven marketing principles, keep selling to many of them as they move along that road. These regular buyers become your clients.

Some of your customers and clients will tell other people they meet along the way about you. In time, some of these people will knock on your door asking for information. In time, some will leave you. They will try different products and services.

If you have a clear idea of how this process works, then you can ensure that your marketing has the maximum effect at each stage of your clients' journey. The objective is to turn customers and clients into advocates who recommend you on a regular basis.

Here, then, are the six steps for creating advocates.

1. Suspect

This is an individual or business you want to sell to. A reasonable number of 'suspects' should be stored in your sales and marketing database. Remember that those with similar needs comprise a market segment.

If you're just starting out, you need to decide which market segments to target. Don't try to sell to them all; that is almost always a certain route to disaster.

If you have an established business, analyse your client list. Break it down into groups of clients (e.g., by industry). You can then start to communicate with these groups in a targeted, meaningful way (*see* Chapter 2.1). In a competitive marketplace this will help you to make your business stand out from the crowd.

Successful businesses offer

specific solutions

to

specific market segments.

---

2. Enquirer

This is someone who has asked for more information. This is a critical stage. You must treat enquirers with care!

When someone says, "Tell me more", you should make the following assessment:

- Can you satisfy their needs?   *Needs*
- Who is the decision-maker?   *Decision-maker*
- When do they want it?   *Timescale*
- Do they have the money?   *Budget*

Your mission is to get more people to say, "Tell me more." If you're targeting your marketing well, these enquiries should be coming from your chosen market segments.

You must get as many of these "Tell me more" conversations started as possible because:

More conversations = more clients

3. Prospect

This is someone who is going through the process of qualifying as a customer. All businesses should have a 'pipeline' of prospective customers whom they've identified, talked to and qualified. Do you have a sales pipeline, written down?

4. Customer

This is someone who has bought from you once. Money has changed hands on a single occasion. There probably isn't a deep relationship (yet). If you've been in business for some time, you might have quite a few 'dormant customers'. If this is the case, go back and start communicating with them again.

Remember that it's **five times less expensive**
to sell to an existing customer
than it is to a stranger.

5. Client

This is someone who has bought from you more than once. There is repeat business. For example, this person has bought multiple consultancy sessions with you, or keeps coming back for more of the same product, or you have cross-sold them other products / services. This means that the relationship has deepened as you've had the time to get to know each other better.

A good example of cross-selling would be when one of your seminar delegates buys your consultancy services.

6. Advocate

This is someone who regularly recommends you and your products / services to other people. Some of your customers and many of your clients should become advocates. You'll also find advocates among your (non-client) friends and acquaintances. (For more on advocates, *see* Chapter 5.5.)

As an exercise, make a list of some of your best advocates.

CHAPTER SUMMARY

Be aware of the steps on the road to advocacy – Keep a list of 'suspects' on your database – Build up and assess 'enquirers' – Create a sales pipeline of 'prospects' – Contact customers – Consolidate the relationship with your clients – Make a list of your advocates

Additional laws

Here are a further 16 client-attraction laws. If you use them, more clients will be attracted to your business. They are divided according to: personal attributes; building relationships; communication; verification; reducing the risk; and completing the circle.

Personal attributes

Integrity

People like dealing with honest, straightforward people. So integrity is clearly good for business. If you do what you say you will do, treat people fairly and are honest in your dealings, the word will spread. People who've bought from you in the past will come back to you. More clients will recommend you.

Creativity

Creativity is a magic marketing ingredient. Creative thinkers can:

- generate new ideas on demand
- see things from a different perspective
- help others to produce ideas
- invent new ways to make money
- produce more sales leads

And that's just for starters!

In a time of rapid change, creative thinking can make all the difference. One of the simplest ways of tapping into your creative powers is by learning creative thinking techniques, such as Mind Mapping (*see* Box 2).

Building relationships

Relationships

It's important to focus on building relationships. Good relationships are built on trust. The foundation of trust is integrity. Given time, these relationships will open doors for you via introductions and word-of-mouth recommendations. They will also enable you to sell new products / services to a growing client base.

> *More marketing = more relationships = more clients*

Networking, in particular, is a great way of building relationships because you are meeting people face to face.

In combination with the rest of the marketing mix, you'll soon find that there are plenty of people to talk to and that the number of clients who come to you will increase.

Politeness

How long does it take to type "Thanks for your e-mail"? Does politeness matter? The answer is, "Yes, it does." People notice these small touches.

Saying or writing "please" and "thank you" doesn't cost anything, but it will help to differentiate your business and put clients at ease. I suggest that you include 'politeness' in your marketing plan and sales training programme.

Database

A sales and marketing database is the foundation of professional marketing. On balance, it's usually better to use an off-the-shelf package than to re-invent the wheel by building your own system or heavily modifying a database not intended to be used for sales and marketing.

Using a database properly involves research, data acquisition, data validation, testing and direct marketing. You should constantly update your database with new information.

Keep all your records in **one database file**.
As time goes by, this will make the data
much easier to work with.

How do you ensure you are working from a 'clean list'? In other words, how can you check that you have accurate data so that you don't keep getting messages such as "Mr Smith no longer works here"? Telemarketing agencies usually do this by calling an entire list to check that the contact information is correct. You could delegate this task to, for example, homeworkers or students on a short-term basis. (In the UK, however, remember to check your list against the Telephone Preference Service, as failure to do so can result in a fine.)

Responsiveness

Be quick off the mark when it comes to responding to current and prospective clients. Ensure you have a way of knowing that a client has called you, so that you can return their call as soon as possible. If you're going to be unavailable for a day or more, let clients know via a brief e-mail.

Communication

Clarity

Tell clients, in detail, why your products / services and your solutions are so good. Don't do what others often do and use vague superlatives about your 'tremendous' business.

In your 'calls to action', tell people precisely what to do next. Don't be vague – spell out what action they've got to take.

Provide accurate facts and figures. This will make everything else you say much more believable and will help you achieve better results with your marketing.

Benefits

Benefits are the real reasons people buy something. For example:

- What do hand-held drill manufacturers really sell? *Holes.*
- What do supermarkets sell? *Convenience.*
- What do manufacturers of expensive sports cars provide? Think about it (and the answer is not "a fast way of getting from A to B").

BOX 10

Listing benefits

Write the name of your business at the top of a piece of paper. Draw a line down the centre. Write 'Features' at the top of the left-hand column. Write 'Benefits' at the top of the right-hand column.

Now write down all of the features of your business in the 'Features' column (e.g., how long it has been in operation, the number of staff, your products / services). Opposite each feature, write down a benefit in the 'Benefits' column. Be careful to write down real benefits.

Refer to your benefits list when you are producing promotional material.

Here is an example:

JOHN SMITH MANAGEMENT CONSULTANTS

FEATURES	BENEFITS
Founded 1992	Put our knowledge to work for you
16 staff	Are always there for you
Specialise in the IT sector	Understand your challenges
Nice people	Provide no-hassle consultancy service
Use the XYZ consultancy system	Use proven methodology that delivers results
Mentoring service	Talk it through with someone who isn't involved in the internal politics

Always focus on benefits that are in the mind of your buyer. If you aren't generating enough sales leads, or if clients aren't buying from you in sufficient quantity, it might be because you aren't promoting the true benefits that address clients' real needs.

You must be clear about the difference between 'features', 'advantages' and 'benefits'. Take, for example, a box of matches:

- a *feature* of a box of matches is that it has a drawer
- an *advantage* of having matches in a box is that they stay safe
- a *benefit* is that the box makes the matches much easier to carry around, thereby adding to their convenience value and giving an instant flame whenever it's needed

The point is that people really only buy benefits, not features. This fact doesn't seem to have filtered down to sales assistants in shops, who often go on and on about the endless features of the cooker / hi-fi / car / item of clothing, but seldom turn these features into benefits.

Repetition

According to marketing lore, it takes seven repetitions before someone will remember a new product name. This is why advertisements are usually run as part of a campaign. The advertiser / advertising agency wants to maximise the number of times that they are seen, in order to hit that magic seven.

On this basis, once you have selected your target audience you should repeat your message over and over to them. Your message will then 'sink in'.

Selling

If you are in the business of sales lead generation you need to understand the principles and psychology of selling. This knowledge will help you time and time again. Sales professionals learn a range of skills, such as the art of listening, how to ask questions correctly, how to highlight the benefits and how to handle objections.

If you don't have a sales background and haven't had any formal sales training, you should invest some time and money in this. At the very least, buy some books on selling. Better still, sign-up for an introductory course on the basics of selling. You'll probably be surprised how much there is to learn!

Verification

Testimonials

Testimonial statements work. Take a look at advertisements for books and films – they often use glowing testimonials from critics. Successful direct marketing companies make great use of testimonials. For decades, marketers have been using testimonials to give businesses credibility.

Surprisingly, many client-based businesses don't use testimonial statements at all, or not enough. After a job well done, ask your clients for a few words of feedback by e-mail or by letter. And note down any unsolicited positive comments that clients make about your business. You can then use the testimonials throughout your promotional mix once you've had approval from your clients to do so.

By the way, if you're concerned about your competitors stealing your clients, don't include the clients' names; just give the job titles and company names.

Reducing the risk

Guarantees

It can be difficult offering a guarantee, but it's worth it. If you offer a guarantee – and are loud and proud about it – you should attract more clients. And if you're good at what you do, which I'm sure you are, few (if any) will ask for their money back.

Try offering a guarantee on one of your products / services. For example, a consultant could offer a half-day consultancy session. The promotional copy would say something like:

> "Guaranteed to get you X result. If we
> don't achieve this, we won't invoice you."

Powerful stuff, isn't it? Think of a guarantee that you could offer. Test it out on a small scale and measure what happens.

Should things go really wrong the buyers will, ultimately, be able to get their money back under the Sale of Goods Act (or similar legislation in countries other than the UK). But it's more likely that they won't buy from you again. Arguably, therefore, if you're not 'loud' and 'proud' about your guarantee, you'll have the legal liability without the benefit.

Completing the circle

Integration

One of the best ways of making your marketing strategy truly effective is to ensure that it's integrated. For example:

- Is your marketing planned and delivered on a consistent basis by one person or the same team of people?

- Are you using your key messages throughout your promotional mix?

- Does your logo appear in the right colours and proportions in all your marketing materials?

- Does all your marketing have a consistent look and feel?

- Do you always use the same graphic designers, copywriters and other marketing services professionals?

- Is each marketing item linked to other relevant items of your promotional mix (e.g., is your website address printed everywhere it could be?)

Testing

Part of the fun of marketing and sales is coming up with a lot of ideas. You will have to generate many ideas before you hit on one or two great ones.

How do you know which ideas are good ones? Test them out! For example, if you've thought of several offers, you could test some out through direct mailshots. You would then ramp up the one that produced the best test result.

Never stop testing, and your advertising will never stop improving.
David Ogilvy (advertising guru)

Follow-up

Regular communication is one of the most productive ways of generating business. A key aspect of this process is your marketing database (*see* page 50). All your clients – current and prospective – should be in there.

As soon as someone buys something from you, drop them a note by e-mail or postcard to thank them. About a week later, send them another note, asking how they're getting on with your product / service. Believe me, they will notice this ('thank you' notes in business are rare, aren't they?). From this point on, write to them with news, special offers, website updates, and so on.

How often should you communicate? I suggest at least once a month, but many highly successful companies get in touch with their clients every week.

The same approach applies to anyone to whom you provide a sales quotation (but who didn't buy from you first time around) and any prospective clients you meet through networking. Keep their names in the database and keep that communication going!

BOX 11

Keep in touch

Many companies spend their entire marketing / sales budget on finding new business. It costs **five times more** to sell to a stranger, however, than it does to an existing client.

So the message is, once someone has bought from you, **keep in touch**!

- Keep in touch with 'suspects' so that they think of you when they're ready to buy

- Keep in touch with clients so that they keep coming back for more

People can quickly forget what they hear or read. Make sure they don't forget you by developing a good communication strategy. This is good practice from both a memory and a brand-building point of view. Consistent communication *alone* is a key differentiation strategy (most businesses don't bother).

Here are some figures to think about.

- If you keep in touch, a one-off sale turns, on average, into **three sales a year**

- Once someone becomes a regular client, the chances of them recommending you to friends and colleagues **triples**

See the article 'Love your customer' on www.nigeltemple.com

Tracking

Always find out what led to a sale. Then you can discover what's working and what isn't. You'll need patience because it'll take some time to figure out what works best for you and your business. But the wait will be worth it! In addition, when it transpires that someone has referred you, it's an opportunity to thank that person.

CHAPTER SUMMARY

Display integrity – Become a creative thinker – Build relationships – Be polite – Keep an up-to-date database – Respond quickly – Be clear and accurate – Think 'benefits' – Repeat your key messages – Learn the secrets of professional selling – Ask for and use testimonials – Offer guarantees – Integrate your marketing strategy – Test your ideas – Follow up and keep in touch – Analyse what led to a sale

Stage 4

USE INTERNET MARKETING

Think of your website as a marketing hub.
It is the centre of your marketing communications
machine. Your website must attract the right type of
client and help you to start building a business
relationship with them.

Does your website generate business for you? I've asked hundreds of business owners and marketers this question. Generally, the answer is, "No."

A website has become essential in the 21st century. Prospective clients are unlikely to take you seriously if you have a poor website or – gasp! – no website at all.

In 2000 I launched my first website. It was quite an ordeal. Today, getting a website up and running is a simple task. Since 2000 I have taught thousands of delegates the joys of internet marketing, and shown numerous clients how to improve their websites. (For more detail on internet marketing, refer to my second book in the Temple Marketing Series, *How to Make Your Website Generate Business*; *see* Appendix 3.)

Don't get sidetracked with the technology. What really matters is how to transform your website into a client magnet. To help you focus on this, here are 10 rules of internet marketing:

The rules of internet marketing

1. Your objective is to generate a regular flow of sales enquiries from your website.

2. Ask current and prospective clients what they'd like to see on your site and in your e-newsletter.

3. Test, test, test.

4. The internet is unique because it is interactive. Make your site as interactive as possible (e.g., provide forms for people to fill in, use auto-responders and include an automatic sign-up process for your e-newsletter; *see* Chapter 4.2).

5. Create a site that is helpful for clients. The best way to do this is to provide useful and up-to-date content.

6. Update your site regularly. The search engines will notice and will rank it higher. Prospective clients will also notice, which means they're more likely to get in touch.

7. You have four seconds to make a positive first impression on people visiting your site for the first time. The site must look professional and be easy to understand, or your visitors will disappear in a click!

8. Keep everything simple. Don't use 'all-singing-all-dancing' software for the sake of it.

9. Choose promotional techniques that support your website.

10. Don't expect instant success. Persistence is what counts.

Make your website work hard for you

Here are some ideas to help make your website work harder for you and to generate more sales enquiries.

- *Display your **telephone number** on your homepage.* Ideally, put it in the upper right-hand corner (advertisers will tell you that this is a 'hot spot' on a page). Position your telephone number in the same place on every page of your site.

- *Display the words **'E-mail us'** on your homepage,* just below your telephone number. Some people like to call, others like to write.

- *'Cloak' your e-mail address, using ASCII character code, to **stop spam**.* This can be done by a technical friend or a web development agency.

- *Include **meta tags** within the HTML of your website.* This helps search engines find you. Note, however, that not all search engines use meta tags.

- *Provide **useful, interesting content** for site visitors.* If your site simply tells visitors how wonderful you are, they are less likely to visit it than if you give them something interesting to read and to recommend to others. The key is to produce significant amounts of new material on an ongoing basis.

- *Don't be shy about putting **offers** on your site.* The name of the game is to get a response, and offers often do the trick.

- *Place an **e-newsletter sign-up form** on every page of your site.* 'Permission-based' e-mail marketing is a highly effective way of generating business (*see* Chapter 4.2).

- *Produce **information products**.* Examples include a 'hints and tips' list or a buyer's guide. Offer them as free downloads in exchange for the recipient's contact details.

- *Set up **links to other sites**.* This is not as altruistic as it sounds. Some search engines will rank you higher if you provide outgoing links, so your site will be more visible. Also, visitors will see that you've done your homework and will appreciate being recommended to useful sites.

BOX 12

Meta tags

Meta tags are keywords and phrases added to the HTML of a website to enhance search engine optimisation (SEO). There are three types of meta tags:

Title tags: These should refer to the contents of the page. So it is important to have different tags for different pages.

Description tags: These give a description of the page, instead of the rather random wording often featured on a search engine results page.

Keyword tags: Some search engines go through your site and save your keywords in their database. When someone uses that search engine, it refers to this database.

As an example, here are the meta tags on my website:

<title>Nigel Temple's free marketing tips and ideas website</title>
<meta name="description" content="Discover a treasure trove of FREE marketing articles, tips and ideas.">
<meta name="keywords" content="nigel temple, nigeltemple.com, marketing, marketing advice, marketing consultancy, marketing ideas, marketing tips, marketing training, small business marketing, SME marketing, marketing speakers, marketing speaker, creative thinking, Mind Maps®, Mind Mapping, business development">

For more on the mysterious world of search engines, go to www.searchenginewatch.com. If you want to push SEO to its full extent, take a look at Web Position (www.webposition.com), a software package that automates the processes involved in SEO.

- *Get as many sites as possible to **link back to you***. When you have links to and from another site, this is called a 'reciprocal link'. Search engines like reciprocal links.

- *Get into **affiliate marketing***. Affiliate marketing is becoming big business. This is how it works: someone visits your website and sees that you recommend, for example, a book; they click on a link and get taken to, for example, the Amazon site; if they buy the book, Amazon pays you a commission. If you have something you can sell directly from your site (e.g., an e-book), you can set up a network of affiliates linked to you.

- *Place **articles** on other, non-competing sites and in 'article directories'*. Ask them to include a link back to your site.

- *Start **blogging***. A blog (derived from 'weB LOG') allows you to post messages and receive replies, and will help your search engine rankings. You can experiment via www.blogger.com (owned by Google).

- *Find out which pages on your site receive **'unique visitors'***. Use a website statistics package or on-line statistics service to do this. Here are three useful sites: www.sitemeter.com (free), www.coolstats.com and www.webtrends.com (corporate). You can then use this information to design better web pages.

Some observations

Take a look at my website homepage as it looked in mid-2007 (*see* Figure 8). Note that:

- The branding is on the top left (where the eye usually starts on a web page).

FIGURE 8: The homepage on the author's website (mid-2007)

- The phone number and 'E-mail Nigel' are on the top right.

- There are only seven navigation bar items (between five and nine items is best).

- There are a lot of testimonial statements (immediately giving credibility and reassurance to someone who is about to buy).

- The first paragraph describes what I do. Don't make it difficult for visitors to figure this out!

- In the central column is the beginning of an article. This article gives the search engines a lot of material to feed on and gives prospective clients something to get their teeth into.

- At the top of the right-hand column is an offer for a free marketing toolkit.

CHAPTER SUMMARY

Apply the rules of internet marketing – Display contact details on every page – Provide interesting content – Include offers – Send out a regular e-newsletter – Tempt visitors with information products – Set up reciprocal links with other sites – Attract search engines – Get into affiliate marketing – Put articles on other sites – Become a blogger – Use webstats to find out which pages get the most visitors

4.2 | Launching an opt-in e-mail newsletter

Permission-based e-mail marketing can produce outstanding results. It's a great way of keeping in touch with contacts and current and prospective clients. It's either free or low cost, and each e-mail can be personalised.

What is permission-based e-mail marketing? It means that the recipients of your e-mailed marketing material have said, "Yes, I would like to receive this material" (hence the phrase 'opt-in'). These people are your 'subscribers'.

Note that I am *not* talking about spam – unsolicited e-mails from total strangers. Spam is proving to be a real nuisance to many people and is giving legitimate e-mail marketing a bad name. This is a pity because e-mail marketing is such a great way of building relationships and generating sales leads.

You should be aware that the law in many western countries is moving towards encouraging opt-in direct marketing. This type of marketing is highly effective. After all, if you are providing interesting, informative information, most of your target market should be happy to 'opt-in'. By this stage, you'll have created a competitive advantage – that is, 'prospects' and clients who welcome your marketing material.

Key elements of e-mail marketing

The four key elements of e-mail marketing are:

1. Managing your subscription list
2. Building your list

3. Choosing your e-zine / e-shot format
4. Getting the writing done

BOX 13

E-zines and e-shots

'E-zine' means 'e-mail magazine'. E-zines are usually sent out regularly to a wide subscriber base. They contain informative content.

'E-shots', typically, try to sell something, such as a seminar or a product. They are usually 'one-offs'. If you send several e-shots, one after the other, expect a lot of complaints and subscription cancellations!

The focus in this chapter is on e-zines because, although an e-shot can generate business, the smart money is on e-zines. They build relationships, provide something interesting and are (usually) *free*! That's why selling on the back of an e-zine can be such an effective way of generating sales leads.

Managing your subscription list

You have several software options for managing your subscription list:

- Your current e-mail package
- Bulk e-mail handling software
- Sales and marketing databases

E-mail package

You can use your current e-mail package to manage the list (e.g., in Microsoft® Outlook® you can create a new folder entitled 'e-zine list'). When you want to contact your subscribers, you then:

- write your e-zine
- click the 'To' button at the top of the e-mail
- select the 'E-zine list' folder
- highlight everyone on the list
- click 'Bcc' (blind carbon copy)

If you don't click 'Bcc', everyone will see everyone else's e-mail addresses. The unscrupulous might steal these addresses for their own purposes. I still receive e-zines and e-shots from people who seem to be unaware of this.

Find out how to personalise your e-zine (i.e., with 'Hi <First Name>' at the top). When I found a way of personalising my e-zines, response leapt.

Bulk e-mail handling software

Your second option is to use a bulk e-mail handling software program. Two examples of this type of package which can be installed on your computer are:

- *GroupMail* www.infacta.com
  Its key features are:
  - you can set up and send e-zines / e-shots to as many groups as you wish
  - you can personalise each message
  - there's a free trial version

- *EasyMail* www.glocksoft.com
  Its key features are:
  - you can send out personalised e-mails to many recipients at one go
  - it's easy to manage your lists
  - there's a free trial version

Sales and marketing databases

The key issue with these databases is whether or not they allow you to send bulk, personalised e-mails. Do be careful; there are some problems with well-known database packages! (For more on databases, *see* Chapter 3.4.)

Building your 'opt-in' subscription list

As we're talking about 'permission-based' marketing, it's important that all the subscribers on your list have asked to be on it. When you have confirmation that they wish to receive your e-zine, then they are 'opt-in' subscribers. There are many ways to build your e-zine subscription list. Here are a few examples.

E-mail signatures

Your day-to-day e-mails could include information about your e-zine within your e-mail 'signature'. These 'mini adverts' can be in plain text or colourful HTML (as long as the recipient can view HTML e-mails). The way to set this up will depend on the software you use to handle your e-mails.

Here is an example of the type of message you could use:

Subscribe to our e-newsletter!
It's packed with useful tips and ideas.
Click here to find out more.

Signing up non-subscribers

Good e-zines will get forwarded. So give non-subscribers an easy way to sign up, such as including printable instructions and giving them reasons to try you out.

To encourage your existing subscribers to forward your e-zine, at the *top* of the e-zine write something like: "We rely on recommendations to find new subscribers. Please forward this e-zine to a friend. Many thanks for your help!"

E-zine sign-up form

Your website is clearly a great place to promote your e-zine. You can have a small sign-up form on your homepage or you can direct visitors to a separate e-zine sign-up page. You should have an e-zine sign-up form (or a link to the form) on every page of your site.

When new subscribers sign up, they should immediately be taken to a 'thank you for signing up' page. Send them a welcome message. Include something useful in this message, such as some relevant tips or advice, or an article.

People are wary of getting unwanted spam, so do highlight your privacy policy. It should state that you won't sell your e-zine subscribers' e-mail addresses.

BOX 14

Some tips for building your e-zine list

- The fewer mandatory fields there are on your e-zine sign-up form, the more subscribers you'll get.

- If you're e-mailing people already on your e-zine list, it looks odd if you promote your e-zine to them. So have two e-mail signatures, one for current subscribers and the other for prospective ones.

- Send prospective subscribers an instant 'thank you' gift for signing up (e.g., something with a tangible benefit, such as a free article or e-book).

- Ask e-zine publishers who target the same market as you do to promote your e-zine, and tell them that you will do the same for them.

E-books

Produce a free e-book on a hot topic. E-books are usually produced as Adobe® PDF files. Provide the files as free downloads from your website and promote them in your e-zines. In turn, promote your e-zine in your e-book! As e-books are passed around the internet, they can become highly effective marketing vehicles.

You could also produce a paid-for e-book. Start by carrying out a survey to see what would interest your subscribers (visit www.surveymonkey.com). You could also run an on-line survey, and refer to it in your off-line promotional mix. Either way, you won't need large numbers of completed survey forms to assess what topics would be popular.

Then compile the e-book and, in it, promote your free, content-rich e-zines. Promote the e-book on-line and off-line. If you market to businesses, most companies / departments now have a corporate credit card that they can use to pay for the e-book. Usually sold for anything between £5 and £70, paid-for e-books can help to generate cash.

Articles on other websites

Submit articles to relevant, non-competing websites with the express purpose of generating new e-zine subscribers. Webmasters might allow you to include details of your e-zine at the end of the article, enabling readers to subscribe then and there. It's a good idea to use a unique e-zine subscription address so that you can track which articles are producing the best results.

If you're not allowed to promote your e-zine in the article, offer further information via a hyperlink that takes the reader to a page with information on your e-zine – and an e-zine sign-up form.

Choosing e-zine formats

The format you choose for your e-zine is very important. There are three options:

1. Plain text
   Advantages: inexpensive to produce; quick to download; more likely to get through corporate firewalls; focuses on words
   Disadvantages: no colour or graphics; not 'corporate' in look or feel

2.	HTML without graphics
	Advantages: use of colour; more coherent layout; quick to download; easy and inexpensive to produce; easier to track responses
	Disadvantages: might not get through corporate firewalls; some subscribers won't be able to view HTML

3.	HTML with graphics
	Advantages: looks good; opportunity to use creative graphics; has a 'corporate' look and feel
	Disadvantages: could hit firewalls; some computers can't read HTML; can look awful if all the graphics don't download

I recommend that you start with a plain text e-zine. It is the least time-consuming option and stands the greatest chance of getting through. Then, once the e-zine is established and you're more familiar with how it all works, you could produce an HTML version as an option.

Getting the writing done

Don't try to write your e-zine in one sitting. Instead, open a file and gradually add bits and pieces to it that might interest your readers. When you start producing your e-zine, you'll then have some raw material ready and waiting.

E-zines don't have to be very long, a few hundred words at most. If writing isn't something you enjoy, consider hiring a freelance writer to help you write the e-zines or edit your rough drafts. (For more detail on e-zine content, refer to my third book in the Temple Marketing Series, *How to Write Compelling Marketing Words*; *see* Appendix 3.)

The Marketing Mentor

Marketing ideas from Nigel Temple   **April 23rd 2007**

In this issue

Download a marketing plan
template (no charge!)

Create a clear vision of
your successful future

Increase your promotional
mix and activity

Marketing Masterclass

Download a marketing plan template (no charge!)

Entrepreneurs, directors and marketers fall into two groups. I wonder which you belong to?

The first group doesn't really know where they are going. They are looking for 'the next customer', or 'more sales'. They certainly work hard enough - but not on the right things. As they are short term focused, let's call this group the 'Tacticals'.

The second group are the 'Strategics'. They take time-out to think about the future of their enterprise. They have a concise plan. As Dwight D. Eisenhower said: "Plans are useless, but planning is indispensible."

Click here for a marketing plan template. You are welcome to copy and paste this directly into your wordprocessor.

Hi Megan

Within this edition, there is a link to a marketing plan template - which you are welcome to copy.

The Marketing Mentor is read by over 2,000 opt-in subscribers. This time, there are three steps to producing a successful 'Marketing Future' (cue spooky music!).

I will be taking the attendees of my next Marketing Masterclass through this three step process. Step 1: Create a clear vision of your successful future (see the article below). Step 2: Produce a concise marketing plan. Step 3: Increase your promotional mix and activity (Big Time!).

All the best, Nigel

PS There is a 2 for 1 offer for the Marketing Masterclass as well as for tomorrow's Copywriting Seminar (click here to find out more). Only four places left. Now that we are all publishers, compelling writing is more important than ever!

Create a clear vision of your successful future

Do you know what your 'future enterprise' is going to look like? At given milestones (i.e. three years from now), what will it turnover? What will your profitability be? How many customers / clients will you have? And what sort of lifestyle will it allow you to create?

A clear picture of what you want: does this sound daunting? Well, the answer is "Yes" for most people on our planet. If you want your enterprise to succeed - you must have a clear vision of where you are going. As the business owner or key marketing person - this is critical. Vision creation is a right brain process; all the millionaires I have worked with are outstanding in this area.

If you are able to attend my next Marketing Masterclass, then you are welcome to share your vision with me, at the event. And I will give you some feedback / insights that may help you!

Increase your promotional mix and activity

There are over 250 ways to promote your business. Take a moment to list your 'promotional mix'. You can select from the following categories:

* Advertising * Alliance marketing * Corporate clothing

FIGURE 9: An excerpt from the author's e-zine, *The Marketing Mentor*. The e-zine focuses on low-cost ways of generating sales leads

BOX 15

A secret formula

Here is my 'secret formula' for successful e-zines.

Send your subscribers interesting, informative and useful tips and advice based on what they want to learn about. If you do this once a month, they won't forget you. And they won't mind if you also try to sell them something.

CHAPTER SUMMARY

Use permission-based e-mail marketing to keep in touch – Think about ways to manage your 'opt-in' subscriber list – Develop your subscription list – Make sign-up forms easy to use – Launch an e-zine – Choose a workable e-zine format – Promote your e-zine via clients, e-books and articles – Take time writing e-zine content – Send out a monthly e-zine

Stage 5

USE LOW-COST PROMOTIONAL TECHNIQUES

Now that you have built your online presence, you must get out there and build a positive reputation for your business. Interestingly, some of the most effective promotional techniques for client-based businesses are either free or low cost. Stage 5 describes these techniques. Use as many as you can and use them consistently, month in, month out. You should spend up to a quarter of your time on promotion.

Some of my best friends are professional networkers. They make the effort to attend business gatherings and talk to lots of people. Without exception, their businesses are thriving. They know that it's worth keeping on attending chosen networking groups, as it takes some time for people to get to know you and understand what you do. There's a good example described in Box 16.

Try to attend networking events every month. There are numerous networking opportunities out there. They include Chambers of Commerce events, professionals' meetings, and events arranged by business networking organisations.

Here are some networking ideas to think about and apply.

Plan ahead

If you don't plan ahead, you could waste valuable time attending networking events. It's important to:

- consider what your objectives are (e.g., how many events to attend monthly and how many new contacts you want to make)

- find networking groups populated by prospective clients and / or people who can reach these clients

- ensure that you have plenty of business cards

- print some postcards about your business (using a size that fits easily into jacket pockets, handbags, etc.)

BOX 16

A networking success story

I met Phil Hawthorn at a networking event in 1996. We were the only people who showed up! I got on with him immediately and we both thought that the situation was hilarious. It turned out that he'd just set up a management consultancy and training business and was busy networking in order to build contacts and clients.

He became such an assiduous networker that before long it seemed that everyone I met in the Thames Valley knew him.

One of the networking groups that Phil had joined was for human resources (HR) professionals – one of his target groups. At the first two meetings he talked to an HR professional who, on both occasions, asked him what he did.

At the third meeting, she was talking about a team challenge she was facing and Phil suggested a solution. She looked startled and said, "Tell me what you do again?"

Phil was subsequently awarded a contract to help solve the team problem.

Prepare a networking pitch

When you meet people at a networking event, they will inevitably ask what you do. You then have a few fleeting moments to say something interesting and memorable. You are hoping that they will say, "Tell me more", hence the need for a networking pitch.

When I ask people at networking events what they do, there are always some who:

- are inconsistent in what they say
- include lots of 'ums' and 'ers'
- ramble through a lengthy description

Take a moment to write down what you would say at a networking event when you are asked what you do. Then say it, without looking at what you've written. Did you stumble? It's a simple exercise but most people do stumble a little.

BOX 17

Experimenting with your networking pitch

Here is a networking pitch I used to use:

"My name is Nigel Temple. I'm a marketing consultant. I teach 2,000 people a year how to get results from their marketing."

This produced only a moderate response. The problem with it is that it is feature based (i.e., 2,000 people a year). So I tried a benefit-based pitch:

"My name is Nigel Temple. I'm an independent marketing consultant. I help businesses to find more clients. I teach a proven system for generating a river of enquiries. Once implemented, this low-budget system will work for years to come."

This brought a much better response.

For many years, marketing gurus have talked about 'USP' statements. The 'Unique Selling Proposition' concept was invented by Rosser Reeves, an American copywriter. Most of my clients, however, struggle to come up with a really original USP. They find it easier to produce a networking pitch than a USP statement.

The best way to develop an interesting and memorable networking pitch is, first, to come up with the keywords that describe your business. This tells people *what you do*. Then come up with the keywords that describe the results you generate. This tells people *what you deliver.*

Use these keywords to write your networking pitch. Once you have written it, you can use it in many ways and in many situations.

Overcome nerves

Being confronted by a room full of strangers can be pretty nerve racking. To overcome nerves, try this:

- as you are travelling to the event, visualise a successful networking experience; imagine meeting lots of interesting people with whom you'll have great conversations

- before you enter the room, take some long, deep breaths; remember that most of the people in the room are as nervous as you are

- once in the room, don't drink too much coffee or alcohol – and keep smiling!

Work the room

Don't get trapped talking to people you know. Circulate around the room, talking to as many people as possible. All you have to do initially is catch someone's eye and smile; most people will return the greeting.

Spend most of the time listening. Practice asking open questions – how, what, why, when, where, who, which – because this will get the other person talking.

Try to unearth a need or a problem they might have, and write it on the back of the business card they've given you.

Follow up on networking events

When you return to your office, send your new contacts a note or e-mail as soon as you can after the event. Try to help them in some way with a challenge they are facing.

One way of keeping in touch is by suggesting that they subscribe to your e-zine.

Identify the hubs

Some people you meet when you network will be well connected. I think of these people as 'hubs' (like the hub of a bicycle wheel, with spokes radiating from the centre). If just a few 'hubs' decide to put you in touch with their contacts, your business could take a leap forward.

Figure 10 shows the relationships between a diverse group of people. The thicker the line, the stronger the relationship.

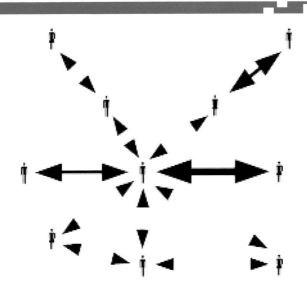

FIGURE 10: A relationship web, with the thicker lines indicating stronger relationships

The person in the middle of the figure is clearly a 'hub', as he knows everyone else, with two exceptions. But he can introduce you to these two people in one step, through an intermediary contact. If you were networking in the circles in which he moves, he'd be well worth knowing!

Consider forming your own network

Think about forming your own network. How about a Lunch Club? Or a Breakfast Network? You could make it for people in your town, for example, or for people in the same industry. Don't think in terms of 'competition'; rather, think in terms of learning opportunities and potential marketing partnerships.

Like most marketing activities, networking takes time. It is an inexpensive tool in the promotional mix, however, and will at least get you out of the office!

CHAPTER SUMMARY

Attend networking events regularly – Plan ahead – Prepare a networking pitch – Overcome nerves – Work the room – Ask open questions – Follow up new contacts immediately and keep in touch – Identify and get to know the 'hubs' – Consider forming your own network

5.2 Using direct mail

The postman brings me some very entertaining direct mail. Being in the marketing business, I study the envelopes and sometimes open them. Often, they are:

- incorrectly targeted (I don't need a stair lift – yet)
- misspelt (how many ways can you spell 'Nigel'?)
- badly designed
- poorly written

Direct mail can be an effective way of building awareness of your business and creating clients. Many business people object if you send them unsolicited e-mail, but direct mail doesn't seem to bother them in the same way. It can be well targeted and because it has (or should have) someone's name printed on it, it is likely to be seen.

Added advantages of direct mail are that it doesn't involve the emotional drain of telemarketing and it's less intrusive than phoning.

Set specific targets

Before you do a mailshot, you should set targets for the number of:

- people you want to reach
- responses
- successes (appointments, sales, etc.)

Keep a record of the number of people to whom you've sent the mailshot.

Review your results. Talk them through with someone. It's amazing what you can achieve if you set clear targets.

Database and data protection

It's very important to choose the right database when you're direct mailing. (For more on sales and marketing databases, *see* Chapter 3.4.)

Data protection legislation is an ever-changing field. The easiest way to find out about the current state of affairs is to search the internet.

Mailshot content

It is critical that you get the content just right, or your mailshot – on which you've spent valuable time and money – will be in the bin within seconds of its arrival. You can get it right by:

- aiming your mailshot at the right people – that is, the decision-makers in your chosen target market segments

- taking time to think about who you're communicating with and how to get their attention (there are different 'buttons' to press, for example, if you're communicating with a managing director rather than a financial director)

- thinking in terms of the issues which these job titles encompass

- tailoring your opening words to the recipient's particular situation and needs, and showing that you have experience in helping other people to address these needs

- grabbing the recipient's attention straight away (with direct mail, you have only a few fleeting seconds to grab someone's attention before they switch off, so those opening seconds are critical)

- writing compelling copy (*see* Chapter 6.1)

- including a story about helping a similar company solve a problem – everyone likes good story – and asking if they'd be interested in finding out how you did it

- scattering testimonial statements in the mailshot; testimonials are a great source of credibility

- including a strong call to action (ask them to 'ring this number or send an e-mail'; don't leave it to the recipient to figure out what to do next)

Another approach is to send interesting items of information you've come across in the media or which have been brought to your attention. As long as the material is relevant and interesting, it will get the recipient's attention. Include a hand-written note along the lines of: "I thought that you might find this useful."

Following up a mailshot

There's a rumour going around that you should follow up all the mailshots you send out. I don't know who started it. It's not true.

By all means follow up some of them. But think about this: if you ring and say that you are following up a mailshot, what are people likely to say? Almost certainly, "What mailshot?" The human brain can think about only a handful of items at any one time (apparently, men can think of seven things simultaneously, and women nine).

Asking about a mailshot is likely to start the conversation off on a negative note. But if you insist on following up mailshots, don't mention them in your opening gambit.

CHAPTER SUMMARY

Set specific targets for your direct mailing – Choose the right database – Check data protection legislation – Aim the mailshot at the right decision-makers – Make it grab their attention immediately – Write compelling copy – Include a story – Use testimonials – Include a call to action – Don't necessarily follow up mailshots

5.3 Organising events

Standing in front of an audience is one of the best and most cost-effective ways of generating new business. For many people, though, nerves and anxiety pose a challenge. With preparation and practice, however, they can overcome this challenge. It's well worth the effort.

Learning to speak in public is a highly valuable skill. It will serve you well on many occasions. Do give it a try if you haven't done so already.

Choose a topic

What could you talk about? Begin by thinking about your target markets. What are they interested in? Think in terms of both 'old faithfuls' and 'hot topics'. For example, e-mail marketing was a 'hot topic' in 2006, but that 'old faithful' – how to generate more sales leads – will always be of interest.

Once you have a list of potential topics, focus on the ones where you have first-hand experience and know a lot about. If you talk about things you really understand, your knowledge will shine through and your performance will be more engaging.

Prepare, prepare, prepare

The key to great presentations is preparation. It always has been and it always will be.

Here are five key points you need to consider:

- When will the presentation take place?
- Who will you be talking to?
- What do they want to learn?
- How long will your presentation be?
- Where is the venue and what is it like?

A little research beforehand to answer these questions will go a very long way. When you've answered the questions, start working on your presentation.

Work on the presentation

There are three components to a successful presentation or speech: the opening; the main course; and the big finish.

The opening

You must grab their attention as soon as you get up to talk. A good way to do this is to ask a question which is relevant to the members of the audience. For example: "How many business owners do we have here today?" Each person in the audience must think about the question, which means that you've immediately engaged them. Then a forest of hands will go up. And off you go.

The main course

Are you good at telling jokes? Not many people are. The reason seems to be that when we start telling a joke, it dawns on us that we can't remember how the joke proceeds. Then the real trauma hits us when we realise that we can't remember the punch line!

For presentations, I recommend using a Mind Map®. One of the great things about Mind Mapping is that it jogs the memory about the key points. In Chapter 2.1 we talked about this technique and how useful it is in sorting out your thoughts. For your presentation, you should 'Mind Map' the key points (*see* Figure 11). Once you have a grip on the 'milestones' of your presentation, which are on the branches of the Mind Map®, the rest will follow.

Using a Mind Map® will mean that:

- you won't have to read your speech (which usually bores an audience)
- you'll feel much more confident when you get up to talk
- your nervousness will subside
- everything else will fall into place

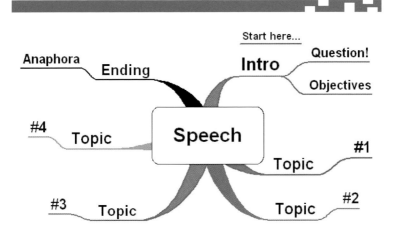

FIGURE 11: Using a Mind Map® to deliver a speech

Does this sound too good to be true? Well, try it and find out for yourself. (For more on Mind Mapping, *see* Box 2.)

Some presentation tips

Overcome nerves. Everyone feels nervous before giving a speech, but there's a difference between the tingling sensation of anticipation and a pumping heart and sweating hands. Before the speech, visualise yourself talking confidently to an interested audience. Just before you begin, take a dozen deep breaths. This will calm you.

Keep moving. There are two reasons why you should move around. First, it's boring to watch someone giving a presentation from one spot (from behind a podium, for example). Second, you will release some of your nervous energy.

Be enthusiastic. There is nothing so dull as listening to an unenthusiastic speaker. Be passionate about your subject (no matter how dry it might be). People respond to enthusiasm like bees to pollen.

The big finish

Leave the audience on a high note! Conclude with something dramatic. Quotations are a good way of concluding your speech.

Another good way is to use 'anaphora' – the repetition of the same word or words at the start of consecutive sentences. Winston Churchill studied what the Ancient Greeks thought about public speaking. One of the techniques he borrowed from them was anaphora, which creates a natural, recognisable rhythm. The audience can hear the rise towards the finale. Here is an example:

If we can all consider these issues
If we can all work together as a team
If we can all put our differences to one side
Then I know that we will undoubtedly succeed

Note that there are three consecutive repetitions of "If we can all". Professional speakers know all about the magic of the number three. For some reason it always sounds good in a speech.

I'll end this discussion of anaphora by telling you that **this technique** has soul. **This technique** touches our emotions. And **this technique** is a great way to finish a speech!

Find presentation opportunities

It's a good idea to open a file with information about organisations that might require your services as a speaker. Once your 'radar' is attuned in this way, you'll start to find all sorts of speaking opportunities.

To get you started, here are some suitable organisations: business associations; business clubs; Chambers of Commerce; institutes; networking organisations; special interest groups; and large companies. Always go for those organisations that are populated by members of your target audience.

Organise your own event

Instead of being a speaker at someone else's event, you could host your own event. Although this is a time-consuming and sometimes fraught exercise, it can generate a lot of business. You'll need to decide whether to make it free or paid for.

Free events:
> *Advantage*
> • No barrier to people saying, "Yes, I'll come along"
>
> *Disadvantages*
> • No perceived value
> • There could be a high no-show rate
> • You'll have to pay for the marketing and the venue

I've experimented with both free and paid-for events and have found that it's a good idea to hold a free event from time to time. I ask each participant to bring a colleague (from my target market). This 'bring a guest' approach puts me into contact with people who wouldn't otherwise know about my business. It also generates considerable word-of-mouth marketing for me.

You can use free events to showcase some interesting material, such as a new service you're offering (without giving too much detail away). Events can also be used as part of a 'two-step' approach, such as promoting a paid-for seminar or your consulting services.

You should also experiment with organising paid-for seminars. If they run, you'll make money. If they don't, it won't cost you a great deal if you choose venues that don't charge too much for cancelled events.

Get people to attend

An ideal way of inviting people (for free) is via your own e-mail list. (For more on e-mail marketing, *see* Chapter 4.2.)

You could also find a non-competitor who has an e-mail marketing list aimed at the same target market as yours. Your mission would then be to persuade that person to send out an invitation to your event – ideally, with an endorsement! Why would they do this? The answer is that you could send out some marketing material, endorsing them. (*See* reciprocal marketing partnerships, Chapter 3.2.)

Another approach is to use a 'two-for-one' offer – two people for one event. The real bonus of this approach is that delegate A, who really wants to attend, persuades delegate B (a friend or colleague) to come along. You would almost certainly not have met delegate B in other circumstances. And both A and B could end up becoming clients!

Select your venue

A key issue in venue selection is their cancellation policy. Ideally, you want a venue that won't charge you if the event doesn't run. The second-best option is that you lose your deposit (typically, about 25%; obviously, the smaller the better) if you have to cancel the event within X days / weeks of the event.

Arrive early

Always arrive as early as possible at the venue, at least an hour before you're due to speak. Check all the equipment.

Make sure that the seating is as perfect as it can be. Sit in a few of the chairs that the audience will be using, to see the view that they will have. If there are technicians involved, introduce yourself to them and find out their first names.

The power of public speaking

Robert Brown is a management consultant. He saw me deliver marketing speeches in a city centre restaurant to a networking group one evening and then in a church hall to another group. Subsequently, he got up early in the morning to attend some breakfast networking groups I was addressing, once in a golf club, another time in a hotel. He said later that I provided him with a motivational burst for the day ahead.

I began to look out for him, sitting at the back of the room and smiling at my manic delivery. Gradually, he began to refer clients to me for a 'chat'. I was happy to help, offering free one-hour consultancy sessions on Mondays. (I kept this up for a year, until I became inundated with clients.)

Of the dozens of business owners I met through Robert, I sold one-off marketing sessions to half a dozen of them and was awarded marketing projects with three companies. When I totted up the fees from these clients and the people they referred me to, the total exceeded £50,000. Naturally, I have been happy to refer numerous clients to Robert.

The key issue is the act of recommendation. If you've been recommended, then you're already half way to winning the business.

CHAPTER SUMMARY

Choose a topic of interest to your target audience – Talk about what you know – Prepare, prepare, prepare – Plan the beginning, middle and end – Use Mind Mapping – Find presentation opportunities – Host your own events – Try both free and paid-for events – Find ways to get people to attend – Select your venue – Arrive early – Recognise the power of public speaking

The topic of this chapter is PR – meaning, in this context, 'Press Relations'. PR is important for client-based businesses because it raises your profile and enhances your credibility. The process of writing PR material will also make you think and could lead onto bigger things, such as books.

PR is seen mainly as an awareness-building technique, and the sales leads that come from PR tend to be high quality. On a space comparison basis, PR is *five times more effective* than advertising. When you think about it, this isn't really surprising. After all, do you buy magazines and newspapers to look at the advertisements?

All advertisements have clearly been produced and paid for by a particular organisation to get their message across. When you read them, you know that you're being 'sold to' and you therefore put the necessary 'filters' in place. Conversely, magazine and newspaper articles have been independently researched and written by journalists – haven't they?

The answer is, by and large, "Yes". This is especially the case for the national press and the broadcast media. But it's quite common to see articles in trade and professional magazines and newspapers that have been written by companies. And pieces on new products and people are nearly always the result of PR efforts. Beyond this, you might be quite surprised at how much an influence companies, charities, the government, special interest groups and others have on the 'independent' media.

Build your media contacts list

The place to start is with your media list. Begin by collecting relevant magazines and newspapers. Look for the colophon, the section that gives the name of the editor, journalists and others, and their contact details. A key item of information is the editorial e-mail address. This might be the e-mail address of the editor, or something like editorial@xyz-magazine.co.uk

Many publications have their own websites that contain e-mail addresses. Be aware, though, that some of these sites are run as separate entities to the printed version of the publication, so you may have to contact them separately.

Another way to obtain media contact information is to visit the reference section of your public library, where you should find some media reference guides (e.g., *Benn's Media* and *Willings Press Guide*; for details of the latest editions of these guides, *see* Appendix 3).

Put the e-mail addresses you've gathered into your e-mail software, or into your marketing database if you can use it to send e-mails. You'll then be able to start sending press releases and other material to the right people.

Press releases

The staple diet of the PR world is the press release. A press release is a news announcement sent to a selection of media. There are four main reasons for sending out press releases:

- *New product / service.* This type of release is almost guaranteed to get some coverage in the trade press. Most trade journals have a new products section and information from press releases fills about 80% of the space.

- *Improved product / service.* If your business frequently launches new products, that's great from a PR point of view. If you don't fall into that category, it's still likely that you will improve, update or enhance your products / services periodically. Look for the news value and send out a press release.

- *Events.* If you're organising an event, such as a seminar, send out a press release about it.

- *Website.* There's no point sending out a press release saying that you have a new website, as it won't get any coverage. If you have something useful on your site, however, then by all means send out a press release about it.

Writing a press release

Huge swathes of the content in trade publications are drawn from press releases. Here is a step-by-step guide to producing one.

- Begin by asking yourself: Is the subject newsworthy?

- Think in terms of 'news value'. If, for example, you have half a dozen potential press releases on your hands, in what order do you send them out? Generally, the ones with the most news value should go first. By the time you reach numbers five or six, something else of greater news value might have occurred.

- At the very top of the release, write: 'PRESS RELEASE' and the date.

- Write a headline that clearly says what the press release is about. For example, are you launching a new service? If this is the case, say so. Although editors will almost certainly change your headline, use it to convey your message to them quickly.

One press release = one subject
Don't try to combine several announcements
in a single press release.

- Give the gist of your story in the first sentence. Cover the key points in the first paragraph. (Once you've got press coverage, compare your press cuttings with the original press releases. How often did they use the first paragraph? How often did they use only the first paragraph)?

- Each paragraph must be able to stand alone. Editors quite often delete whole paragraphs at a time, so whatever is left must still make sense.

- If you refer to other companies (e.g., clients or suppliers) in your press release, make sure that you have their permission to do so.

- The ideal number of pages for a press release is one. Go for two pages if you feel you really must. There's seldom a good reason to go to a third page.

- Write a standard 'boiler plate' paragraph giving an outline of your business. Describe what your business does, when it began, how big it is (turnover, staff, etc.), where you operate, recent developments and anything else you feel is relevant. Mark the paragraph 'For editor's information' and put it at the end of all your press releases.

- Always put contact details at the end of your press releases. The recipients need to know your name, job title, telephone number, e-mail address and physical address. Having said this, it's quite rare for the press to contact you, particularly in the early days, so don't sit by the phone waiting for a call.

Send your press release

Increasingly, the media will accept press releases that have been sent by e-mail. I suggest that you create a separate e-mail address folder in your e-mail system, entitled 'Media', or add media contact addresses to your sales and marketing database if you're able to send personalised e-mails from this software. Then start adding those e-mail addresses.

Some media organisations still insist on receiving press releases by mail. In this case, use your own letterheads, with double-line spacing and big margins. It is much easier for editors to edit copy when there is plenty of space on the page. Print on only one side of the paper. I would recommend putting press releases unfolded into large envelopes. This makes it physically easier for editors to deal with them.

Writing articles

Much of what has been said about writing press releases applies to writing articles. The style and format of an article, however, differs from that of a press release.

There are three types of articles:

- *Technical*. An article about how a service or product has been developed

- *Business*. An article about your business (e.g., a description of what is unusual about it)

- *Case study*. An article about a happy client

Technical and business articles

Decide who is going to be credited with writing each article. Generally, if there is a lot of product / company information in the article, it comes over better if a 'third party' name is at the end. The reader will then assume that it's been independently written. If, however, the article deals with an industry issue, for example, then you or a member of your staff should be named as the author.

Case study articles

If you write about a client using your product or service, this is a case study. Ensure that you have your client's permission for this. Send your client the final copy for approval / comment before it's sent to the media.

Here are some questions you could ask in a case study interview:

- Who / what did you use before?
- Why did you change?
- How did you go about searching for a new product / service?
- How many suppliers did you look at?
- Why did you choose us?
- How is it all going now?
- What benefits are you getting from using us?
- What do you think of us / our product / our service?
- What plans do you have for the future in this area?

BOX 20

Some tips on writing articles

- Every article is a story and people like stories. As in all good stories, you should have a beginning, a middle and an end – set the scene, delve into the intricacies of the plot, and write a happy ending.

- Think hard about the headline and the first paragraph. You have to grab the reader's attention!

- Edit and proofread your work carefully.

- Refer to the earlier section on 'Writing a press release' (*see* page 102).

Place your articles

Always place an article before you write it. The phone call would start something like this:

> "Hello, my name is ... from ... (*the name of your business*). I wonder if you could tell me what your policy is concerning submitting articles to ... (*the name of the publication*)?"

If they're not interested, you could, depending on how the conversation is going, try to interest them in something else – a new service you're launching, or an interview perhaps.

If they do seem interested, then tell them briefly about your idea for the article. Assure them that the article will be objective, and not full of references to your business. If they still seem interested, ask them how long the article should be, whether they want photographs and when they want the article by.

Sometimes, the editor will ask you to put it all in writing. It's surprising, though, how many will agree to look at your article after just a brief phone call.

Recycle your articles

For most people, writing an article takes a fair bit of time and effort, so it's a shame to see it printed only once. Yet you can't afford to anger your hard-won press contacts, and an editor won't be happy if a rival magazine publishes your article shortly after it's appeared in his or her publication.

When you're researching the article, try to get enough information for several articles. For example, research the technical, business and human interest angles of the subject.

Having placed the article for the first time, you can then produce a different version for another publication.

With subsequent versions of the original article you can, for example:

- change the headline and the first and last paragraphs
- change the first line of each paragraph
- use different photographs
- find a magazine in a totally different media segment, and hence with a different readership
- go for a different geographical area
- try again a year later

Get the most out of your articles

Once an article has been published, try to get the maximum value out of it.

Start by asking the magazine or newspaper how much it would cost for them to provide 'reprints' for you. Usually, this is quite inexpensive because they would have already created the artwork for the article. You can then use the reprints in direct mailshots, as give-aways at events, and so on.

With the publisher's permission, you could also reproduce the article as a PDF that can be downloaded from your website.

BOX 21

Articles can produce great sales leads

After sending a series of e-mails to magazine editors suggesting subjects for an article, one of them asked me to write about low-cost marketing. I wrote 800 words and a few months later it appeared in print, with a photograph of me.

Soon afterwards, the managing director of an electronics company called. Would I meet him to talk about his marketing strategy? At the time I was so busy I had to decline. He left further messages for me and eventually I agreed to meet him, a couple of months after his first call. When we met, he said that he'd been reading the articles on my website and they were very helpful.

When I e-mailed a quotation to him, he accepted by return. Over a 4-month period, I produced a marketing plan, helped him to re-think his website and had a series of marketing brainstorming meetings. It was an enjoyable project. And it wouldn't have come my way if I hadn't written that article!

CHAPTER SUMMARY

*Put PR high on your list – Build up your media contacts
– Be clear about the reasons for sending press releases
– Decide on the news value of press release subjects – Set up
a system for sending press releases – Think about writing
articles for the media – Place an article before writing it
– Recycle your articles – Get the most out of your articles*

Referrals are the recommendations that your contacts and clients give you, the names of people they suggest you approach. They are a great way of getting business. They are free, and you don't have to spend time finding them.

The trouble is, the process is very hit and miss. Is there some way you can turn an intermittent trickle of referrals into a regular stream? The answer is, "Yes, there is".

Deliver effective solutions and good service

If your product / service really 'does the job', people will start to recommend you to their contacts. Great service is a marketing strategy all on its own. It generates positive word-of-mouth. Many successful companies have made 'exceptional service' part of their culture.

It takes only a relatively small percentage of clients to start talking about your enterprise for there to be a snowball effect. So it's worth finding out what your clients really think about you. The easiest way to do this is to get someone else to ask them. That way, they are much more likely to reveal their true feelings.

Cherish your advocates

An advocate is someone who recommends you to other people (*see* Chapter 3.3). About 5% of people are natural advocates. They simply enjoy the act of recommendation. But you won't know who your advocates are unless you ask the right questions. For example, in response to a sales enquiry, the right question is, "I wonder how you found us?"

The rule, therefore, is that you should always try to find out where sales enquiries come from. If the lead is from an advocate, make sure you thank him or her. You could send an e-mail, but because advocates are so important, a nice touch would be to send them a personal, handwritten note, perhaps on a postcard.

You'll find that a natural advocate will know other natural advocates. They seem to be on the same wavelength. So yet another reason to cherish your advocates is that they will spread the word through their network of advocates.

Transform unhappy clients into advocates

When problems occur, as they certainly will, sort them out immediately. Don't let complaints and awkward situations fester. If you take the time to find out who is dissatisfied

BOX 22

Keeping track of advocates

In your sales and marketing database create a file entitled 'Advocates'. Whenever you learn that a client or contact has recommended you, put a note to this effect in this file. This will ensure that you have up-to-date and easy-to-access information about your advocates.

with your product / service, all sorts of interesting things will happen. For example:

- the unhappy client will stop telling people how awful you are (it's worth the effort for this reason alone!)

- if they are happy with the outcome, this is a real 'story' that many of them will willingly tell their contacts and friends

- they'll come back to you and, typically, will be more loyal to you than if there had been no trouble in the first place – amazing, but true

Having solved a problem, always follow up to see what the client thinks of the solution. Remember that their feelings are the real issue here.

Ask for referrals

Why do so many people find it hard to ask for referrals? The answer is the fear of rejection. If this sounds like you, here are some ideas that could help.

- Write down the exact words you would use when you ask for a referral. If you write it down, you can work out exactly what to say.

- Practise with different words and phrases and experiment with different versions, to see which ones work best.

- Ask for advice (everyone likes to be asked for their advice). You could say: "Could you give me some advice? In your opinion, which other businesses should I contact in this area / industry?" Say that you'd like to write to them, which means that you need addresses. (If you work in the UK, don't forget the Data Protection Act.)

- Practise asking for referrals in front of a mirror or with a colleague acting the part of the client (actors never go on stage without rehearsing their lines, and you shouldn't either).

- Experiment with asking for referrals by e-mail. This gets round having to ask people face to face, and you can also get the words just right.

- Soon after you've completed some business, ask for a referral. Get into the habit of doing this.

- Let your clients know that you welcome referrals. One way of doing this is to add a few words to your e-mail signature (*see* Chapter 4.2). After your contact details in the signature, for example, you could write: "By all means tell a friend about me. Thank you!"

- Set yourself targets for referral numbers. Try, for example, to generate four referrals a month. Remember, what gets measured, gets done.

Always thank people promptly when they've given you a referral, regardless of whether or not you get any business from the referral.

Before you contact someone to whom you've been referred, do some research. The easiest way of doing this, probably, is to look at their website. This information will help you to form a better rapport when you make contact.

BOX 23

Make referral requests part of customer care

A good approach is to make referral requests part of your customer care programme. Having completed an assignment, e-mail or give out a 'feedback form'. On this form ask your clients to tell you what they think about your product / service. At the end of the form, ask if they would be so kind as to give you some names of other people to contact.

This way, you won't have to go through the awkwardness of asking for referrals; it'll just become part of the way you conduct your business.

Get promotional items passed on

A different approach is to have something specific to give to your clients for them pass on to their contacts. The most obvious item is business cards. You could also send reprinted magazine articles (*see* Chapter 5.4). From time to time I give my clients and contacts three postcards with something useful / informative printed on them (*see* Chapter 3.1) and ask if they would be kind enough to give them to three of their contacts.

Spread the word

On average, we each know about 250 people. This includes immediate family, our wider family, school friends, college / university friends, neighbours, work colleagues and business contacts. Depending upon your stage in life and personal interests, more groups of people could be added to this list.

So when you market to people and seek referrals from them, remember that each person you contact will probably know several hundred other people. This is why word-of-mouth marketing can work so fast. In order to tap into these contact chains, you must keep marketing, keep networking and keep asking for referrals.

Whenever you get the chance, make a point of telling people what you do. This is when a networking pitch can come in handy (*see* Chapter 5.1).

BOX 24

Six degrees of separation

According to word-of-mouth legend, you can reach anyone else on the planet through a chain of only six people.

For example, if you wanted to get your pen into the hands of the President of the USA and you live in the UK, it might go something like this:

1. You give the pen to someone you know in the UK…
2. …they send it to a friend in the USA
3. That person sends the pen to someone else…
4. …who has a contact in Washington
5. That person knows someone who works in the Senate…
6. …who gives it to the President

Good stories

People love stories. Good stories can spread like wildfire. Is what you do or offer so interesting that people will want to talk about it? Some people are lucky enough to be in a fascinating business, but most businesses don't fall into this category, which means that you probably need to put your creative hat on!

Here are some ideas that could get people talking:

* hold an event, such as a seminar or an open day, and encourage everyone who has registered to invite a friend

* invent a gimmick that will start tongues wagging (for example, produce postcards with useful lists of dos and don'ts)

* surprise your clients with something extra, for free, just for being your client

This reminds me of a story I heard about an antiques shop. The owner would occasionally send a customer a book about antiques, as a 'thank you'. Often, the lucky customers would return to the shop to thank the owner. "And while I'm here," they would find themselves saying, "would you tell me about that interesting object in your window?"

Team involvement

If you work in an organisation, word-of-mouth marketing and referral generation should be discussed several times a year. Don't leave it to chance. Teach other people what you've learnt. Consider having targets for referrals and giving prizes for the team members who do best in this area.

CHAPTER SUMMARY

Recognise the value of referrals – Build referrals through effective solutions and great service – Cherish your advocates – Transform unhappy clients into advocates – Practise asking for referrals – Get promotional items passed on – Spread the word – Generate a good story about your business – Get everyone involved in word-of-mouth marketing

Stage 6

WRITE COMPELLING WORDS

Writing is a critical 21st-century marketing skill. This is largely due to the rise of the internet as a communications tool. You must be able to produce clear, compelling copy if you are going to attract more clients.

Producing effective copy

Are you a writer? To a great extent, the success of your marketing communications rests on your writing abilities. Some of my clients and seminar delegates love to write. Others prefer to give the task to someone else, such as a professional copywriter.

In marketing, 'copy' means 'marketing words', so 'copywriting' is the process of writing words that promote a business, product or service. If you are going to write your own copy, you need to learn professional copywriting skills.

Here are some of the promotional tools where good writing skills are critical:

- Advertisements
- Brochures
- Direct mailshots
- e-shots
- Flyers / leaflets
- Newsletters
- Postcards
- Press articles
- Press releases
- Websites

Here is the five-part structure for an effective promotional piece, based on the AIDCA model:

1. The headline (or opening line)   *Attention*
2. Product description   *Interest*
3. The offer   *Desire*
4. The guarantee   *Conviction*
5. Call to action   *Action*

This model can deliver excellent results. Give it a try!

BOX 25

The AIDCA model

In order to get good response rates to anything you or your copywriter writes, follow the AIDCA model:

Attention   **I**nterest   **D**esire   **C**onviction   **A**ction

Potential clients lead busy lives and are inundated with marketing messages, so you must get their *attention*. When you've done this, you must spark in them an *interest* in what you're saying, generate a *desire* to learn more about your products / services, create *conviction* that you're a credible supplier and get them to take *action*.

An attention-grabbing headline

The headline is the most important item in a promotional piece. It is the gateway through which readers choose whether or not to enter. It carries your message into the readers' minds. And it entices them to read the rest of your copy.

On average, five times as many people read the headline as read the body copy. When you have written your headline, you have spent 80 pence out of your pound.

Advertising guru David Ogilvy was said never to have written fewer than 16 draft headlines for an advertisement. He would show the headlines to colleagues. A select few would then be shown to the client. This is a great approach.

John Caples, an American copywriter and advertising authority, said, "If you create a good headline, your task is more than half completed. It will be a relatively easy matter to write the copy. On the other hand, if you use a poor headline, it doesn't matter how hard you labour over your copy because your copy will not be read."

A headline tip: Use questions in your headlines. Questions engage the reader. They can be used to create highly effective headlines.

A benefit-loaded product description

Begin with the strongest benefit of your product / service. Tell the reader what this benefit will do for them. Don't assume that they'll figure it out for themselves.

Throughout your copy, write in the 'language of benefits'. Always describe the benefit of any feature you mention. If you're short of space, forget the features and focus on the benefits.

I'm often asked whether it's better to write short copy or long copy? Common sense suggests that short copy must work best. Surveys show that, with regard to sales letters, 95% of people think one page is better than several pages. But is this right?

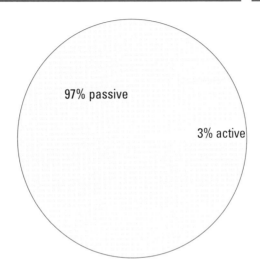

FIGURE 12: The active / passive percentages of the market at any one time

The circle in Figure 12 represents a market that you are targeting. At any one time, most people in this market (97%) won't (currently) want your product / service; this is the 'passive' group. But a small group of people (3%) will be thinking about buying your product / service; this is the 'active' group.

If you send out long copy, it will therefore probably go unread by 97% of the market. The 'active' people, however, will typically read all the information they can find. So at this stage of the buying cycle, long copy can pay dividends. If the copy is filled with compelling reasons to buy from you, so much the better! When people are about to make

BOX 26

An AIDCA-based promotional piece

(ATTENTION – HEADLINE)

Marketing Seminar: How to transform your website into a customer magnet which attracts visitors and delivers sales leads!

(PRODUCT DESCRIPTION – TO GENERATE *INTEREST*)

A step-by-step process for attracting more business: Discover how to get more website visitors and how to generate more sales enquiries. This seminar is crammed with practical tips and techniques which you can put to use immediately.

We will discuss a variety of effective internet marketing strategies, with a focus on client / customer attraction. We will tell you the secrets which create a river of relationships, interest, desire and purchases. You're welcome to ask questions about any aspect of internet marketing.

Special guest: During the presentation, Darin Brockman, MD of BCL NuMedia, will give top tips for internet marketing. www.bcl-numedia.com

(AN OFFER CREATES *DESIRE*)

Two for one offer:
Two delegates can attend for the price of one!

Verbatim will be there, talking about their professional telephone answering service. "They are the perfect companion to your website. Verbatim has created more time for me – to plan and deliver an even better service. In addition, my clients are now able to reach me, wherever I am! " Jennifer Smith
www.ThePhoneAnsweringService.co.uk

Times
6:00 pm – 7:00 pm: Networking.
7:00 pm – 8:30 pm: Presentation in the Studio Theatre.
8:30 pm+: Networking, so do bring business cards!

Venue
Norden Farm Centre for the Arts, Maidenhead, Berkshire
Click the above link for a map.

Registration
Simply reply to this e-mail with the words: "Yes please" at the top.
Or call our office on 12345 678910. Or simply make a payment within
this page: click here to read all about it.

(A GUARANTEE CREATES *CONVICTION*)

Guarantee
If you are not delighted with what you learned, we will refund your
money within a week of the event. No questions asked.

Tickets
Tickets are £XX each + VAT. You can pay by cheque or debit/credit card.

(CALL TO *ACTION*)

Register now!
The seminars are popular and tend to sell out quickly. Why not register
now to ensure your place(s)?

All the best and thank you for reading this far!

w: www.ntmkgsem.com
e: info@ntmkgsem.com
t: 12345 678910

a buying decision, they will hang on your every word. And these are the people that matter to you now.

So the answer is, write long copy. Not only is it what the 'active' group wants, it also means there's more room to provide all the details. When potential buyers are ready to buy, they want to know the details.

Use sub-headings to break up your copy. This enables readers to scan through it easily and find the parts that interest them.

A compelling offer

Offers are a great way of attracting attention. (For more on offers, *see* Chapter 3.2.)

A solid guarantee

If you have a bold guarantee, you'll be 'lowering the hurdle' of doing business with you. This is a great reassurance when the buyer is on the cusp of making a decision. When people buy from you for the first time, they could well be a bit nervous about spending their money on your product / service. A strong 'no questions asked' guarantee will make it easier for them to say, "Yes". (For more on guarantees, *see* Chapter 3.4.)

Other forms of reassurance to potential buyers include testimonial statements, case studies, and facts and figures (e.g., "Feedback shows that 94% of our clients are delighted with this service").

A call to action

End with a 'call to action'. For example, ask the reader to call a telephone number or send you an e-mail. Some people like to phone, others like to write – cater for both groups.

CHAPTER SUMMARY

Improve your writing skills or use a professional copywriter – Follow the AIDCA model – Match the structure of your promotional piece to AIDCA – Write several headlines and choose the best one – Use the 'language of benefits' to describe your product / service – Create desire with an offer – Give a strong guarantee – End with a call to action

Stage 7

TAKE ACTION!

Results will come to those who take action. Don't wait for
the perfect moment: it will never come. Start using the ideas
in this book today. Start doing something now.
Don't wait. Just start.

mplementing your marketing strategy

The real challenge now is to *take action*. Now that you've read this book, you have to find the time to implement the ideas. So reach for your diary and schedule time to:

- plan your marketing
- do your marketing

Do you remember this in Chapter 2.1?

Annually:	Spend one or two days on marketing planning
Quarterly:	Spend half a day reviewing your marketing plan
Monthly:	Devote an hour or two on marketing thinking and planning
Daily:	Do some marketing

Mark these 'appointments' in your diary, for the next three months.

In addition, every day do whatever you can to move your marketing plan forward, even by one small step.

On the page opposite is a commitment you should make. Photocopy it and display it where you can see it.

On pages 132–136 is a checklist of 70 things to do to get more clients to come to you. Tick the box when you've taken action. Depending on the nature of your business, not all the items in the list will apply to you, so adapt them where necessary.

I will move

my marketing forward

every day

CHECKLIST

Create a compelling vision
- [ ] 1.   Create a compelling vision of your client-rich future.

Focus on adding value
- [ ] 2.   Describe your value proposition.
- [ ] 3.   Find more ways to add value.
- [ ] 4.   Focus on quality.
- [ ] 5.   Deliver outstanding service.

Be committed
- [ ] 6.   Write a concise marketing plan.
- [ ] 7.   Write down specific goals, using the present tense (e.g., "I have X clients creating an annual revenue of £Y.")
- [ ] 8.   Revisit these goals on a regular basis.
- [ ] 9.   Diarise the days when you'll review your plan over the coming months.
- [ ] 10. Get up 20 minutes earlier three times a week to work on your client-attraction ideas.

Stand out from the crowd
- [ ] 11. Study your competition.
- [ ] 12. If you want to be remembered, don't just copy. Do something different (if they zig, then you zag).
- [ ] 13. Be passionate. Passion connects you with people.

Set prices
- ☐ 14. Rethink your pricing.
- ☐ 15. Don't quote hourly or daily rates. Focus on value-related project fees.

Be brain friendly
- ☐ 16. Appeal to the imaginative right brain, with professional design.

Write good copy
- ☐ 17. Appeal to the logical left brain, with well-written copy.
- ☐ 18. If you don't like writing, get some help.

Become the guru of your marketplace
- ☐ 19. Demonstrate your expertise.
- ☐ 20. Produce helpful, useful, 'how-to' material.
- ☐ 21. Educate your market.
- ☐ 22. Talk to journalists.
- ☐ 23. Become a public speaker.
- ☐ 24. Launch an events programme.
- ☐ 25. Write in-depth website content.
- ☐ 26. Publish a book.

Rethink your website
- ☐ 27. Does it need a design makeover?
- ☐ 28. Does it appeal to your chosen market segments?
- ☐ 29. Is it interactive?
- ☐ 30. Find out about search engine optimisation.
- ☐ 31. Use blogging to raise awareness and increase your search engine rankings.
- ☐ 32. Launch a client-focused e-mail newsletter.

Build a low-cost promotional machine
☐ 33. Increase the number of ways that you promote your business.
☐ 34. Use as many 'marketing-for-free' techniques as you can (e.g., e-mail marketing, press releases and referrals).
☐ 35. Experiment with client-attraction techniques.

Network, network, network
☐ 36. Join three networking groups, at least one with on-line networking facilities.
☐ 37. Become active within these groups.
☐ 38. Write a networking pitch, then get out there and start using it.
☐ 39. Attend a networking event at least once a month.

Put relationships before money
☐ 40. Build relationships continuously (more relationships = more clients).

Build a database
☐ 41. Use a sales and marketing database to keep track of your contacts.
☐ 42. Keep this information up-to-date.
☐ 43. Whenever you meet a new contact / potential client, key their details into your database.
☐ 44. Back-up your database regularly and keep abreast of data protection legislation.

Improve your written communication

- ☐ 45. Use proven copywriting formulae.
- ☐ 46. Write at least four headlines per piece, then choose the best one.
- ☐ 47. Use short words, short sentences and short paragraphs.
- ☐ 48. Get someone else to proofread your work.

Sharpen your selling skills

- ☐ 49. Use a professional selling process.
- ☐ 50. Become a world-class listener.
- ☐ 51. Be aware of body language.
- ☐ 52. Attend a sales training seminar once a year.

Respond quickly

- ☐ 53. Respond as fast as you can to new enquiries.
- ☐ 54. Reply to e-mails first thing in the morning.

Use a phone answering service

- ☐ 55. Throw out your answering machine.
- ☐ 56. Employ a service where real people answer your phone when you can't.

Build on success

- ☐ 57. Wake up dormant clients.
- ☐ 58. Experiment with new promotional techniques.
- ☐ 59. Try new offers.
- ☐ 60. Find new distribution channels.
- ☐ 61. 'Productise' your services.
- ☐ 62. Launch a follow-up system.
- ☐ 63. Ask everyone for referrals.

Delegate tasks

- [ ] 64. Recognise that you can't do it all.
- [ ] 65. Outsource some marketing tasks, such as web development, direct mailshots and PR.

Find a marketing mentor

- [ ] 66. Find a marketing expert to keep you on track. Meet monthly to discuss your marketing plan and methods.
- [ ] 67. Form a MasterMind group (6–8 people) and meet once a quarter.

Measure your marketing

- [ ] 68. Always ask how prospective clients found you.
- [ ] 69. Use this information to fine-tune your marketing.

Generate new ideas

- [ ] 70. Having read this book, brainstorm 100 ways to improve your marketing.

APPENDICES

APPENDIX 1
Analysing your competitors

Create a detailed profile of your main competitors – say, the top six. Also gather a reasonable amount of information on other competitors.

Then use this information to help you to decide on market positioning, which benefits to promote, where to offer your products / services, and what promotional mix to use.

Here are some of the key points to include in the profiles of your competitors:

Competing businesses
- Competitor's name
- Physical address
- Website address
- Annual report / financial information
- Profiles of directors and key executives
- Mission statement
- Corporate objectives
- Corporate strategies
- SWOT analysis

Their marketing strategy
- Positioning / USP statement
- Niche / vertical market strategy
- Product / service sets, features and functionality

- Product / service literature
- Pricing
- Geographical coverage
- Channel marketing strategy

Their promotional mix
- Examples of advertisements, press cuttings, direct mail, internet marketing, etc.

Your response
- An outline of your competitive response to each of the key competitors
- Q&A sheets, giving answers / responses to competitive issues

APPENDIX 2
Glossary of terms

adding value   Creating additional value for your clients (e.g., extra services)

advantage   An aspect of a product / service which makes it more attractive / useful (e.g., an *advantage* of having matches in a box is that they stay safe)

advocate   Someone who willingly recommends you to others

affiliate marketing   Revenue sharing, typically between websites

AIDCA   Attention, interest, desire, conviction, action

anaphora   Repetition of a word or phrase at the start of consecutive sentences, to create emphasis

article directories   Websites which contain submitted articles

benchmark competitor   A competitor who has reached a position you want to reach

benefit	The real reason behind the purchase of a product / service (e.g., a *benefit* of a box of matches is that it delivers an instant flame)
blog	Derived from 'weB LOG', a person's web-based journal
boiler plate	Standard text at the end of a press release, describing the entity that sent the release
brand	An identity that encapsulates what a business, product or service stands for; ultimately, a brand is a promise
branding	The process of creating an identity for a business, product or service
client	Someone who buys your products / services regularly
cloaking	Disguising your e-mail address (or other information) from spam spiders / bots; cloaking can be done using ASCII character code
colophon	The section in newspapers and magazines that lists journalists' contact names and details
competitive analysis	A detailed study of your main competitors

copy	Marketing words (i.e., the text for marketing materials such as mailshots and advertisements)
copyright	Legal protection for the fair use and reproduction of original material
copywriting	Writing marketing words (i.e., writing the text for marketing materials such as mailshots and advertisements)
cost-plus pricing	Where suppliers add up all their costs and add on a fixed profit margin
customer	Someone who buys your products / services once
data acquisition	Obtaining information for marketing purposes (from a list provider and / or ongoing marketing initiatives)
data validation	Checking a database for accuracy
differentiation	Making a business, product or service stand out from the competition
direct marketing	Sending marketing materials (such as mailshots) directly to prospective customers
elevator pitch	A brief statement which tells people what your business is and what it delivers

e-mail signature   The standard text at the end of an
                        e-mail message with the sender's
                        name and contact details; it can also
                        contain promotional messages
                        (e.g., for the sender's e-zine)

e-newsletter   An e-mail sent regularly to a list of
                        subscribers, containing news,
                        information and promotional
                        material about a business, products
                        or services

e-shot   An e-mail, sent to subscribers or
                        sometimes sent 'cold', which is
                        trying to sell something

e-zine   An e-mail magazine containing
                        news, information and promotional
                        material about a business, products
                        and /or services (like an e-newsletter)

feature   An attribute or characteristic of a
                        product / service (e.g., a *feature* of
                        a box of matches is that it has
                        a drawer)

HTML   HyperText Markup Language (the
                        computer language of the internet)

hyperlink   A link between one element in an
                        electronic document to another
                        element in the document or to
                        another document

IT   Information technology

language of benefits	Words describing what a business *delivers*, not just what it *does*
layout	Arrangement of text and illustrations in print or on screen
list provider	Commercial enterprise supplying mailing lists
mailshot	Direct mail letter, leaflets or postcards
marketing plan	A detailed written strategy for selling products / services (distinct from a business plan)
media list	A list of the names of journalists in various media
meta tags	Keywords and phrases added to the HTML of a website to help with search engine optimisation
Mind Map®	A graphical thought-organisation strategy, invented by Tony Buzan
networking pitch	A brief statement which tells fellow networkers what your business is and what it delivers (*see also* elevator pitch)
opt-in	In the context of websites, where a reader (e.g., of an e-newsletter) decides (opts) to become a subscriber and joins the e-mailing list

PDF	Portable Document Format, created by Adobe®, allowing files to be shared so that everyone sees the same thing
permission-based marketing	Marketing communications sent to people who have agreed to receive them
pitch	Formal presentation of information about products / services to a prospective client
positioning	Customers' / potential customers' perception of a business, product or service in relation to competitors
press relations (PR)	Managed communication with the media
press release	An item of news value sent to people on a media list
promotional mix	The variety of ways a business uses to communicate with its target markets (e.g., advertising, internet marketing, networking, press relations)
prospect	A potential customer who has shown interest in your products / services
Q&A	question-and-answer
reciprocal link	Mutual links between two websites

reciprocal marketing partners (RMP)	Businesses serving the same target markets and collaborating on their marketing exercises
reciprocity	The philosophy of 'give to get'
referral	The act of recommendation
sales lead	An enquiry from a prospective customer
sales pipeline	A list of prospective customers
segment	In the marketing context, a group of people with shared needs
search engine optimisation (SEO)	Making a website as visible as possible to internet search engines
SME	Small to medium-sized enterprise
strapline	A line of text associated with a business, usually appearing beneath its logo
suspect	A person or business likely to be interested in your products / services
SWOT	Strengths, weaknesses, opportunities, threats
tags	*see* meta tags
telemarketing	Telephone-based research, data acquisition and communication

Telephone Preference Service (TPS)	UK government initiative to try to stop unsolicited telephone sales calls
testimonial	A sentence or two of positive feedback from a satisfied customer or client
trade press	Business journals and magazines
Trojan horse	A free or low-cost product / service that establishes a new business relationship
turnover	Gross revenue, before costs and taxation
Unique Selling Proposition (USP)	A proposition, unlike any other, which differentiates a business, product or service
value proposition	The benefits that a business offers, clearly defined in a brief statement
vertical market	An industry with an added-value progression from raw materials to the finished product (e.g., the automotive industry, which starts at the bottom with mining and progresses towards the top – a car)

APPENDIX 3
Selected references and useful websites

References

Bird, D. 2000. *Commonsense Direct Marketing*. Kogan Page, London, UK

Buzan, T. and Buzan, B. 2006. *The Mind Map Book*. BBC Active Books, London, UK

Buzan, T. 2006. *Use Your Head*. BBC Books, London, UK

Black, J. 1994. *MindStore*. Thorsens, London, UK

Caples, J. and Hahn, F.E. 1998. *Tested Advertising Methods*. Prentice Hall Business Classics. Prentice Hall, New York, USA

Girard, J., with Brown, S. 2006. *How to Sell Anything to Anybody*. Warner Business Books, New York, USA

Hawkins, D.R. 2005. *Power vs. Force*. Hay House, London, UK

Ogilvy, D. 2003. *Ogilvy on Advertising*. Prion Books, London, UK

Sayce, K. 2006. *What Not To Write*. Words at Work, London, UK

Temple, N. and Brockman, D. 2008. *How to Make Your Website Generate Business*. Words at Work, London, UK

Temple, N. 2008. *How to Write Compelling Marketing Words*. Words at Work, London, UK

Watts, D.J. 2003. *Six Degrees*. W.W. Norton, New York, USA

Websites

(all preceded by www.)

adobe.com	creators of the PDF file format
blogger.com	blog creation
ecademy.com	networking
glocksoft.com	home of EasyMail
hollispublishing.com/bennsmedia.htm	*Benn's Media*
infacta.com	home of GroupMail
linkedin.com	networking
nigeltemple.com	marketing tips and ideas
searchenginewatch.com	information on search engines
sitemeter.com	webstats
surveymonkey.com	online surveys
webposition.com	search engine optimisation software
webtrends.com	webstats
willingspress.com/default.asp	*Willings Press Guide*
words-at-work.org.uk	books on business writing and marketing
writersandartists.co.uk	writers' and artists' yearbook

INDEX